THE **100** GREATEST
WESTERN MOVIES
OF ALL TIME

Tom Mix LIBRARY OF CONGRESS

THE **100** GREATEST WESTERN MOVIES OF ALL TIME

INCLUDING FIVE YOU'VE NEVER HEARD OF

The Editors of *American Cowboy* Magazine
Foreword by Douglas Brode

TWODOT

GUILFORD, CONNECTICUT
HELENA, MONTANA
AN IMPRINT OF GLOBE PEQUOT PRESS

A · TWODOT® · BOOK

Text design: Sheryl Kober
Layout artist: Melissa Evarts
Project manager: Ellen Urban

Library of Congress Cataloging-in-Publication Data

The 100 greatest western movies of all time : including five you've never heard of / by the editors of American Cowboy magazine ; foreword by Douglas Brode.
p. cm.
ISBN 978-0-7627-6996-4
1. Western films—Catalogs. 2. Motion pictures—Evaluation.
I. Brode, Douglas, 1943- II. American cowboy. III. Title: One hundred greatest western movies of all time.
PN1995.9.W4A18 2011
791.43'65878—dc22

                                                                    2011013058

Printed in the United States of America

10 9 8 7 6 5 4 3 2 1

JUN 3 2011

CONTENTS

FOREWORD

"My heroes have always been cowboys . . ."

—WILLIE NELSON

For a brief time in the nineteenth century (1865–85), the cowboy was simply a blue-collar worker on horseback, somewhat shunned by respectable citizens in northern towns when he arrived with a herd of cattle from Texas. Then something strange and unexpected happened. At the dawn of the twentieth century, Owen Wister published *The Virginian* (1901), and endless movie and TV variations on Wister's profound and romantic themes of the West followed. The cowboy was central to this mythology, and he was transformed in the public's eye from lowly worker to symbol of a noble bygone era. The cowboy became the archetype of our American mythology—a knight without armor (as singer/songwriter Johnny Western put it) who tamed a great land.

The cowboy lives on, of course, but motion pictures manage to capture and deliver his inspiring story to urban masses that seem to need heroes and adventure as an antidote to industrial life. Movies are a medium that by nature calls for action. The word "cinema" derives from the Greek word for movement, and cattle drives, fistfights atop towering cliffs, and shootouts at the O.K. Corral translate well onto the big screen and capture people's imaginations. Western movies speak to audiences of any age, gender, geographic region, ethnicity, or political persuasion. For nearly one hundred years, cowboys have been ubiquitous on the silver screen and even helped found the medium itself and spread its popularity (and America's) worldwide.

In the twenty-first century, the cowboy has become somewhat divisive, representing for some a more conservative ideal to which not everyone adheres. But cowboy movies still unite us all, and great actors, like John Wayne, still inspire love for America and the West. The United States gave rise to other great art forms, like blues and jazz music, but the Western is more personal and somehow universal. The cowboy values of honesty, toughness, and independence are qualities to which we all aspire.

In short, this ranking of the best one hundred Westerns ever made is a primer on heroes and what they represent. The American cowboy is a hero, and watching him in action is the best entertainment we can think of.

—DOUGLAS BRODE

DOUGLAS BRODE lives in San Antonio and is the author of thirty-seven books. He's a frequent contributor to *American Cowboy*, and his next book, *Dream West: Politics and Religion in Cowboy Movies*, will be published in 2011 by University of Texas Press, Austin.

INTRODUCTION

We know the precarious place in which we're putting ourselves by framing a list of the one hundred greatest Western movies of all time. As former *American Cowboy* editor Jesse Mullins said in 2008 when he reviewed the American Film Institute's list of great Westerns, "the Western-watching public would weigh in with its own verdicts, whether pro or con, pleased or not—but never indifferent." Inciting debate, having these discussions—or we daresay mild arguments—and making this list so that readers can revisit old classics or try the unfamiliar and then make their own list is the fun of a project like this. And it's also a great way to keep the genre alive, relevant, and entertaining for generations to come.

The Old West was a tough place to live in, as many a silver screen hero, heroine, villain, or villainess learned to his or her detriment during the past century of movie making. And Hollywood has often been a tough place for the classic Western, or even for the revisionist, modern, or spaghetti varieties. But even though Western movies have been given up for dead many times over the last hundred years, every so often a new great film rises to the surface and to the top of the box office standings. There is something about the genre, something noble, something visceral, that continues to attract audiences from the baby boomers who spent their allowance money on Saturday matinees to new generations of movie fans who are enjoying the fresh air that directors like the Coen brothers are bringing to the genre.

But looking toward the future of the Western—as we write, the critical (and popular) response to the Coen brother's *True Grit*

Children waiting to get into the movies in New Hampshire in 1940 LIBRARY OF CONGRESS

has been overwhelming, and time will tell how many top one-hundred lists the movie will appear on; and trailers for the bizarre mashup *Cowboys & Aliens* may be enticing a new brand of Western audience—we feel it is appropriate to look back on the genre and to feature what we believe are the greatest one hundred (or so) Westerns to come out of Hollywood and elsewhere in the last hundred (or so) years. The opinions about what should be included, indeed about what constitutes a Western at all, are endless and deeply rooted in tradition and a heartfelt love for the heroes of the silver screen. Movies on our individual lists didn't make the final cut, movies beloved by audiences and critics didn't make the final cut, while some movies that other critics hate and despise did. We included so-called "revisionist" movies that reinterpret the West that was—at least according to the interpretation of the West that some of the earliest movies on this list created and that was solidified in the 1950s. We included modern Westerns, love stories, film noir, silent movies, comedies, musicals, and the classic spaghetti Westerns. The list starts with our very favorite in the #1 slot, and the rankings follow from there through our least favorite favorite at #100. Because we couldn't help ourselves, there's also an appendix with a few more. And included in our list there are also five (or more) movies that you've probably never heard of, much less seen. We've tried to make a point of calling extra attention to these unsung gems of the genre.

Put together by editors who are movie lovers, but more specifically Western movie lovers and connoisseurs, our list tries to look at the genre as the art form it is, not comparing it with other movies out there. We've tried to make our reasons for including them clear—but we didn't want to give away the endings. Watch these, celebrate these, and by all means make your own catalog of favorites.

—Philip Armour, Editor-in-Chief,
American Cowboy

Monument Valley, Arizona CAROL M. HIGHSMITH'S AMERICA, LIBRARY OF CONGRESS, PRINTS AND PHOTOGRAPHS DIVISION

THE MOVIES

Once Upon a Time in the West

1969; directed by Sergio Leone; written by Dario Argento and Bernardo Bertolucci; starring Henry Fonda, Charles Bronson, Jason Robards, and Claudia Cardinale

Sergio Leone's epic, classic, superlative, masterpiece of a spaghetti Western makes the number one spot on our list with room to spare. Henry Fonda, in a role he was reluctant to take on, gives a brilliant performance against type as the villain. Charles Bronson, Jason Robards, and Claudia Cardinale are fabulous as the mysterious gunman, bandit, and former prostitute turned homesteader. At its heart, this is a classic story of the West, based in a fictional town called Flagstone, which stands in for all the land and water struggles that shaped the history of western expansion. But it's the subplot—the quest for vengeance—that colors this classic of the genre.

When it was released in 1969, *Once Upon a Time in the West* flopped in the United States. Neither critics nor audiences liked the movie much, and Sergio Leone had been hesitant to make the movie in the first place. Leone had intended to retire from Westerns after finishing *The Good, the Bad and the Ugly* but changed his mind when Paramount offered him the chance to work with Henry Fonda and the budget to make the movie he wanted.

Great in its own right, the movie also references the classics *High Noon, The Iron Horse, The Comancheros, 3:10 to Yuma, The Searchers, The Magnificent Seven, Shane*, and other classics as well. Leone's intent was to rework what had by that time become clichés of the genre in an ironic fashion, turning them on their heads while paying homage.

Since its release, *Once Upon a Time in the West* has been routinely named to top-one-hundred lists, not just of Westerns but of movies of all time. *Time* magazine listed it as one of the hundred best films of the twentieth century. And the Library of Congress has included the movie in the National Film Registry. But maybe all of the references to *Once Upon a Time in the West* in other films are now the truest measure of its greatness—from Quentin Tarantino to Baz Luhrman, filmmakers have quoted Leone's masterpiece in their movies for decades.

Desert landscapes and wooden storefronts—the way the Old West lives on screen and in our imaginations PAUL COARTNEY
SHUTTERSTOCK

The Searchers

1956; directed by John Ford; written by Frank S. Nugent and based on a novel by Alan La May; starring John Wayne, Jeffrey Hunter, and Natalie Wood

It's only fitting that one of the top Westerns in this collection would star the greatest Western actor of all time in one of his best performances of his long career. But there's also irony in this selection, which is now recognized by the American Film Institute as the greatest Western movie of all time and one of the top twenty-five movies of all time. *The Searchers* was director John Ford's 115th feature film, and he had already been honored with Best Director Oscars four times by the time this masterpiece appeared, but when *The Searchers* was released in 1956, it was virtually ignored by the critics and received not a single Academy Award nomination.

In the movie, John Wayne portrays a tragic figure, a Civil War veteran who spends years searching for his niece, who was captured by Comanches in post–Civil War Texas. The story, based loosely on a real occurrence, explores issues of racism, sexism, and the darkest results of men's reactions to violence—set against the gorgeous backdrop of Monument Valley's red sandstone formations. And the role is generally considered one of the Duke's finest performances. It wasn't until more than ten years after the movie's debut that it was reassessed by critics and new filmmakers. Martin Scorcese, George Lucas, Steven Spielburg, and Sergio Leone all referenced the movie in their own works.

———•·•———

The song "That'll Be the Day," written by Buddy Holly and made popular by the Beatles, was inspired by a line spoken by John Wayne in this movie.

———•·•———

Monument Valley, Arizona LIBRARY OF CONGRESS

Montgomery Clift and Joanne Dru, *Red River*, United Artists, 1948 MPTVIMAGES.COM

Red River

1948; directed by Howard Hawks and Arthur Rosson; written by Borden Chase and Charles Schnee, based on a story by Borden Chase; starring John Wayne, Montgomery Clift, and Joanne Dru

The opening of the Chisolm Trail in 1867 provides the historical backdrop for this epic tale of rebellion, bitter rivalry, and conflict. Rancher Tom Dunson (John Wayne) and his adopted son, Matthew (Montgomery Clift), are driving cattle to Red River, when Matthew turns against his father, defiantly taking charge of the cattle drive and the men in their employ. It's a retelling of *Mutiny on the Bounty* on the trail instead of the high seas, with Tom Dunson's contemptible authoritarian ways standing in for those of Captain Bligh.

By the time the herd finally makes it to market, the only possible resolution for the two men at the core of the conflict that's accompanied them for months on the trail is a fight to the death. Disaster is averted by a woman named Tess (Joanne Dru) who breaks up their brawl with her gun. At the end, the men reconcile, but it's clear that they had to survive the journey of the trail in order to have any peace together.

Red River featured wildly extravagant production values and cost more than $3 million to make, but the investment paid off. It was one of the top-grossing movies of 1948, and started a five-movie partnership between Hawks (who was also known for the epic *Mutiny on the Bounty* and the screwball comedy *Bringing up Baby*) and John Wayne.

The movie was nominated for two Academy Awards, one for the story and one for film editing. And it's consistently named in the top ten Westerns of all time.

———•◦•———

Gary Cooper was originally chosen to portray Tom Dunson, but refused because he thought the character was contemptible. It became one of John Wayne's best performances. It was Montgomery Clift's first film.

———•◦•———

High Noon

1952; directed by Fred Zinnemann; written by Carl Foreman and based on a story called "The Tin Star" by John W. Cunningham; starring Gary Cooper, Grace Kelly, and Lloyd Bridges

High Noon is definitely a movie of its time, reflecting the climate of 1950s America though set in a time and place that was mostly myth. Written during the McCarthy era of the 1950s (it was Carl Foreman's last film before he was blacklisted), it was loosely based on a 1947 magazine story, "The Tin Star." But it has most often been seen as a commentary on the politics of persecution rampant during the era.

It's a story of a lone marshal who refused help at every turn when a revenge-seeking killer and his gang threaten him, all while the clock on the screen ticks down the hour before the final showdown. The black-and-white film is spare, the fifty-one-year-old Cooper looks ancient, and the lack of typical frontier violence, Technicolor panoramic landscapes, or bands of marauding bandits or Indians sets it apart from the typical "Western."

And it's exactly that spare style, the simple story of a marshal alone against the world when his own town fails to support him, and a brilliant performance by Gary Cooper that have made this a classic.

Eventually, the virtuous sheriff wins out, vanquishing the enemy and protecting the town. And the movie's critical acclaim shows how much it won over the Hollywood audience. It was nominated for seven Academy Awards and won four, including Best Song for "High Noon (Do Not Forsake Me, Oh, My Darlin')" and Best Actor for Gary Cooper.

Grace Kelly, *High Noon*, United Artists, 1952   MPTVIMAGES.COM

Shane

1953; directed by George Stevens; written by A. B. Guthrie Jr. and Jack Sher, based on the novel by Jack Schaefer; starring Alan Ladd, Jean Arthur, and Van Heflin

A timeless classic, a seminal Western, and one of the most successful Westerns of the 1950s, *Shane* is probably best known today for its classic line, "Shane, come back . . ."

Told through the eyes of the young hero, the movie's gorgeous backdrop of the Grand Tetons helps turn what is in actuality a very simple story into a great Western epic. There's a land dispute between a homesteader and a cattleman, a mysterious gunslinger, a funeral on a hill, and enough gunfights and fists flying to satisfy the myth of the Wild, Wild West.

The film received six Academy Awards nominations, though Alan Ladd's brilliant and probably best-known work as an actor was totally ignored. Of its nods for Best Picture, Best Supporting Actor (Brandon de Wilde), Best Supporting Actor (Jack Palance), Best Director, Best Screenplay (by A. B. Guthrie, Jr.), and Best Color Cinematography, it only won for cinematography.

Alan Ladd, *Shane,* Paramount, 1953

Unforgiven

1992; directed by Clint Eastwood; written by David Webb Peoples; starring Clint Eastwood, Gene Hackman, and Morgan Freeman

It's difficult to believe that it was 1992—almost twenty years ago—when this great Clint Eastwood classic was released in theaters—and that it was only the third Western ever to receive a Best Picture Academy Award.

When Munny (played by Eastwood) agrees to take on one last job, he's been a reformed pig farmer in Kansas for years, having given up drinking and gunfighting. Whether he's convinced by the $1,000 reward offered for the deaths of two cowboys who brutally slashed the face of a prostitute or redemption or both, the noir style and moral ambiguity of the film are part of its appeal. Clint Eastwood's efforts result in a tribute to the great films of Sergio Leone and a forward-looking movie that debunks much of the romanticism of the Old West from previous movies and anticipates the gritty look of later movies and TV series such as *Deadwood.*

Nominated for nine Academy Awards, it won four, including Best Picture. Gene Hackman, who gives a brilliant performance as Bill Daggett, won his second Oscar for this film, earning Best Supporting Actor recognition. Released the same year as another epic, *Last of the Mohicans,* the financial and critical success of this movie show how well it held up against a lofty group of peers.

Johnny Guitar

1954; directed by Nicholas Ray; written by Philip Yordan, Ben Maddow, and Nicholas Ray, based on the novel by Roy Chanslor; starring Joan Crawford, Sterling Hayden, and Ward Bond

Many contemporary critics didn't like Joan Crawford's portrayal of the strong-willed saloonkeeper in *Johnny Guitar,* but we still think that this movie has staying power. In 2008, *Johnny Guitar* was selected for preservation in the United States National Film Registry by the Library of Congress for being "culturally, historically, or aesthetically significant," and the themes and the romantic style of the storytelling—as well as the unusual choice of a female lead—give this an unusual degree of interest among the top ten in this list.

Set in an Arizona cattle town, this could be seen as just another Western that features the conflict between the ranchers, the townies, the railroad, and the bandits and stage robbers who roll through town like so many tumbleweeds. In this case, Vienna (Joan Crawford) is also at odds with the old-fashioned values of the town most of the time, and worse—probably to their minds—she's taken up with the stage robber known as "The Dancin' Kid."

Then the eponymous Johnny Guitar strolls back into the saloon, he and Vienna rekindle an old romance, and he ends up rescuing her from hanging later when she's falsely accused of aiding "The Dancin' Kid" in a bank robbery. The mob of townsfolk is egged on by Emma Smalls, a cattlewoman who's always hated Vienna.

Emma, the true villain of the piece, and Vienna overshadow the menfolk in this tale, told with much less realism than many of the era's Westerns but perhaps more effective for all that.

Ben Johnson, Warren Oates, William Holden, and Ernest Borgnine, *The Wild Bunch,* Warner Brothers, 1969, photo by Bernie Abramson MPTVIMAGES.COM

The Wild Bunch

1969; directed by Sam Peckinpah; written by Walon Green, Roy N. Sickner, and Sam Peckinpah; starring William Holden and Ernest Borgnine

Pike Bishop's (William Holden) band is being relentlessly stalked by bounty hunters, and they've reached the end of the line. Set in 1913, *The Wild Bunch* tells of the end of the Wild West—and the end of its rules and codes. And it tells the story of the men who, faced with the end of one lifestyle, have to decide how to make their way under a new set of rules and codes, eventually choosing to make one last, great strike against society before hanging up their guns for good.

When it was released in 1969, *The Wild Bunch* was incredibly controversial because of its shockingly graphic portrayal of violence. But at the same time, director Sam Peckinpah immediately received accolades for making a film that gave a realistic view of that violence in a violent time. The massacres that begin and end the film are two of the bloodiest and most violent moments ever put on film. First the bandits are ambushed after a failed bank robbery, and at the end they're finished off by a savage warlord after being double-crossed in an arms deal.

Peckinpah had previously directed the classic *Ride the High Country*, also about the fading days of the Old West, but he was a veteran of the more romantic epic, as well, having made *Major Dundee* in 1965. *The Wild Bunch*'s stars, including William Holden, Edmond O'Brien, Robert Ryan, and Ben Johnson, were also veterans of movies with a more romantic view of the West.

The film was nominated for Academy Awards for original score and screenplay—but won none. Still, it stands the test of time as a reference for many filmmakers and with a title that's become part of our vernacular.

Bad Day at Black Rock

1955; directed by John Sturges; written by Millar Kaufman, Don McGuire, and Howard Breslin; starring Spencer Tracy and Robert Ryan

Set in post–World War II Black Rock, a little dying town on the Southern Pacific Railroad, this is a thriller/Western that stretches the edges of the genre and lives on as a great film in numerous categories.

When the train stops in Black Rock for the first time in four years, a one-handed man (John Macreedy, played by the inimitable Spencer Tracy) steps off looking for a man named Kokomo, finds a strange and hostile reception from residents, and is told that Kokomo (a Japanese-American interned during the war) no longer lives there.

The townsfolk's explanations of his departure convince Macreedy that something is terribly wrong, and he eventually, and at great risk, discovers the town's secret.

The "town" of Black Rock, Arizona, was built for the film near the Lone Pine railroad station, a stop on the Southern Pacific, but nothing remains of the set today.

Spencer Tracy and Ernest Borgnine, *Bad Day at Black Rock*, MGM, 1955 MPTVIMAGES.COM

Greed

1925; directed by Erich von Stroheim; written by Erich von Stroheim (though credited to June Mathis on screen), based on the novel by Frank Norris; starring Gibson Gowland and Zazu Pitts

Erich von Stroheim's *Greed* is one of the greatest silent movies ever made, a brilliant Western set in San Francisco at the start of the twentieth century, and one of the most legendary stories of filmmaking to come out of Hollywood.

Gibson Gowland plays McTeague, a dentist who used to be a gold miner. His wife, Trina (Zazu Pitts), has just won the lottery and has become obsessed with money, ruining her life, her husband's life, and that of a former lover who also used to be McTeague's best friend.

Von Stroheim filmed on location in San Francisco and in the Sierra Nevada and Death Valley. He attempted to capture every detail of the original novel, and he spent more than half a million dollars in the process, producing a movie that was originally ten hours long. It was eventually cut down to a more reasonable two and a half. Hours of the cut film were destroyed or lost, making it one of the most famous "lost films" in Hollywood history.

When it was first released it was a failure at the box office, but its realism and epic proportions have gained appreciation throughout the years. There are "restored" versions available that attempt to re-create some of the missing footage.

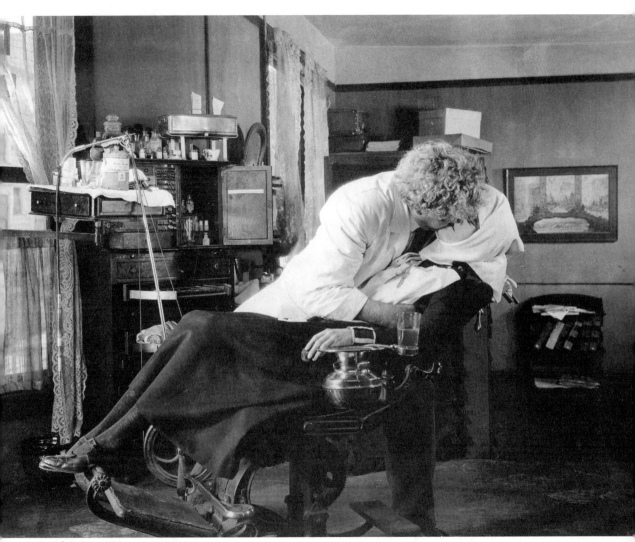

Greed, MGM, 1929 MPTVIMAGES.COM

✳ THE TEN WORST ✳
WESTERNS
❧ EVER MADE ❧

Far be it from us to pass judgment, but since we're already doing that, it seems appropriate to address the bottom of the barrel, the flies in the ointment, the ghastly and the horrifying, the movies that we consider "beyond the pale" in this short list. We recognize that some of these movies are beloved, even award winners—big, ambitious films that simply don't achieve their own hype. But it's our list. Make your own.

Not including the not-even-worthy-of-being-called-a-B-movie drive-in theater nonsense films like *Jesse James Meets Frankenstein's Daughter*, which perhaps have merit within their own genre, these are our picks for the ten worst Westerns made up to now. We're sure some filmmaker will rise to the challenge of being included on this list in the future. *Cowboys & Aliens* comes to mind.

1. *The Way West*, 1967, directed by Andrew McLaglen, starring Kirk Douglas. The best thing we can say about this movie is that it was Sally Field's big-screen debut.

2. *Dances with Wolves*, 1990, directed by Kevin Costner, starring Kevin Costner. Yeah, it won an Academy Award for Best Picture, but its themes set in the West do not make it a "Western."

3. *Doc*, 1971, directed by Frank Perry, starring Stacy Keach. Is it a realistic look at Wyatt and Doc or a pack of lies? Doesn't matter. It's a boring, painful-to-watch movie.

4. *McKenna's Gold*, 1969, directed by J. Lee Thompson, starring Gregory Peck. Omar Sharif is funny as the bandit, Colorado, but we're not sure he meant to be.

5. *Soldier Blue*, 1970, directed by Ralph Nelson, starring Candice Bergen. The scenery is pretty, the violence is horrifying, and the anachronisms abound. If the movie takes place in 1864, why does the protagonist mention the death of his father at Little Big Horn (1876)?

6. *Wild Bill*, 1995, directed by Walter Hill, starring Jeff Bridges. We've seen this described as a "psychedelic Western." Maybe that explains it.

7. *The Quick and the Dead*, 1995, directed by Sam Raimi, starring Sharon Stone. We hate to resort to the same kinds of clichés that plague this movie, but "more style than substance" seems to say it all.

8. *Four for Texas*, 1963, directed by Robert Aldrich, starring Frank Sinatra. Yep, *that* Frank Sinatra. Also Dean Martin and Ursula Andress. It would be funny, if it was funny.

9. *Posse*, 1993, directed by Mario Van Peebles, starring Mario Van Peebles and Stephen Baldwin. We beg someone to make a good movie about the under-recognized black cowboys of the Old West. This isn't it.

10. *The Culpepper Cattle Company*, 1972, directed by Dick Richards, starring Gary Grimes. We can see how you might like this "Western" if you hadn't seen any of the others on our list of the best one hundred. We urge you to run out and do so.

Claire Trevor and John Wayne, *Stagecoach*, United Artists, 1939 COURTESY OF THE ACADEMY OF MOTION PICTURE ARTS AND SCIENCES

Stagecoach

1939; directed by John Ford; written by Ernest Haycox, Dudley Nichols, and Ben Hecht; starring John Wayne, Claire Trevor, and John Carradine

This great study of human nature—a case study in what happens to people drawn together in a pressure-filled situation, isolated from "civilization"—rightfully elevated director John Ford's reputation when it was released in 1939. Its influence showed throughout Ford's career, and its style, substance, and sophistication affected the entire Western movie genre from that time forward.

At the heart of the film is a simple story: A group of nine people, a dance-hall girl, former Confederate gambler, whiskey salesman, young bride, and outlaw characters, traveling by stagecoach through the wide-open American West are threatened by Geronimo and his band. How they react to the situation and to each other is what makes this film one of the greatest Westerns of the twentieth century—the themes of alcoholism, childbirth, greed, shame, revenge, and redemption all take a turn at the forefront of what is also a great adventure story.

Stagecoach was nominated for seven Academy Awards, including Best Picture, Best Director, Best Black and White Cinematography, Best Interior Decoration, and Best Film Editing, winning for Best Supporting Actor (Thomas Mitchell) and Best Score.

———————

John Wayne's Ringo Kid wasn't his first leading-man appearance, but it was his breakthrough role, and he and John Ford would go on to make numerous movies together.

———————

McCabe & Mrs. Miller

1971; directed by Robert Altman; written by Robert Altman, based on the novel by Edmund Naughton; starring Warren Beatty and Julie Christie

Julie Christie is the shrewd Mrs. Miller and Warren Beatty is the dumb but likeable John McCabe—business partners in a whorehouse/bar in the early days of the Pacific Northwest.

The winter landscape underlines the remoteness of the Old West town, which makes it even more striking—and shocking—when a large corporation learns of the mining deposits and tries to buy out everyone in town. In the skillful hands of Robert Altman, the relationship between Mrs. Miller and the hapless McCabe gets a nuanced treatment in spite of the potentially easy exploitation of the "she's smart, he's not" dichotomy between the characters—and the repercussions when McCabe stands his ground against the corporation are heartrending because the audience has become completely enthralled by the deeply flawed and strikingly desperate characters who make up the town.

Julie Christie, probably best known at that time for her role as Lara in *Dr. Zhivago,* and now notable for her turn as Madam Rosmerta in the Harry Potter franchise was nominated for a Best Actress Oscar for her role as Mrs. McCabe and many critics consider it the very best of her work.

McCabe & Mrs. Miller, Director Robert Altman, Warner Brothers, 1971 MPTVIMAGES.COM

No Country for Old Men

2007; directed by Ethan Coen and Joel Coen; written by Ethan Coen and Joel Coen, based on the novel by Cormac McCarthy; starring Javier Bardem, Woody Harrelson, and Josh Brolin

Set in the deserts of West Texas, this Best-Picture Academy Award winner by the dynamic and dark Coen brothers sets a new standard for the Western of the twenty-first century. The screenplay follows the Cormac McCarthy novel faithfully—and the actors live and breathe the print characters on screen in one of the greatest confluences of fiction writing and filmmaking art we've seen for years.

No Country for Old Men reveals the story of an ordinary man who finds a fortune that belongs to drug dealers and ends up on the run for his life from a coldly psychotic assassin. Anton Chigurh, as played by Javier Bardem, is one of the scariest villains in screen history. Hired to recover the money, he strangles a sheriff's deputy, steals a car after killing the driver with a cattle gun, and tracks Llewellyn Moss (Josh Brolin) to Mexico where his pursuit ends in a bloody firefight.

No Country for Old Men was nominated for eight Academy Awards and won four, including Best Picture. Additionally, Javier Bardem won Best Performance by an Actor in a Supporting Role; the Coen brothers won Achievement in Directing (Best Director) and Best Adapted Screenplay. Other nominations included Best Film Editing, Best Cinematography (Roger Deakins), Best Sound Editing, and Best Sound Mixing. The film was also nominated for four Golden Globe Awards, winning two.

The title of the book and the film is taken from the opening line of twentieth-century Irish poet and dramatist William Butler Yeats's poem "Sailing to Byzantium."

They Died with Their Boots On

1941; directed by Raoul Walsh; written by Wally Kline, Aeneas MacKenzie, and Lenore J. Coffee; starring Errol Flynn, Olivia de Havilland, and Anthony Quinn

Errol Flynn and Olivia de Havilland had already proven their mettle as a duo seven times before teaming up as one of the most famous true-life couples in American history. Flynn plays the doomed General George Armstrong Custer, and de Havilland his spunky, adventurous wife, and this movie did a lot to seal the reputation of Custer's last stand as a seminal moment in the history of Western expansion. The only problem with it is that you have to take it as art, not history. The inaccuracies abound.

One of the top grossing films of 1941, the movie follows the Civil War–era romance of Libby Bacon and George Armstrong Custer through their courtship, marriage, and life on the plains. Ironically, it's a piece of the fiction in the story that perhaps comes closest to the truth about what happened to Custer that fateful day at Little Big Horn. Custer's old enemy from his West Point days, the fictional Ned Sharp, is the villain, motivated by greed and jealousy, in the subplot that leads to the takeover of the sacred Black Hills by the white soldiers. In fact, jealousy on the part of some of the other commanders on the scene at Little Big Horn might have affected the outcome of the battle. In addition, the movie version of Custer is sympathetic to the plight of the Native Americans—as he was in life. The real Custer said that if he were an Indian he'd fight the encroaching white expansion, a statement that is repeated in the film, though he never met privately with Crazy Horse as depicted in the movie. At the end of the movie, Custer follows through on his promise to teach his men "to endure and die with their boots on."

———

Following the end of the Civil War, Custer is depicted as a drunkard in the film, while in reality, Custer neither drank nor smoked. After an 1862 drinking binge in which he humiliated himself, Custer vowed never to touch liquor again, and he never did.

———

Will Penny

1968; directed by Tom Gries; written by Tom Gries; starring Charlton Heston, Joan Hackett, and Donald Pleasence

Aging cowboy Will Penny (Charlton Heston) has hired on to patrol a ranch boundary over a long winter. However, when he arrives at the remote cabin that he's been assigned for the duty, he finds that it's already in use by a widow, Catherine Allen (Joan Hackett) and her son Horace (Jon Gries).

BY PAUL/SHUTTERSTOCK

After telling the woman and her son to vacate the property, Penny is attacked by the Quint family, because Penny had earlier killed one of the Quint sons while defending his own companions. After being left for dead, Penny manages to drag himself back to the cabin where, luckily, Catherine is still in residence—since she nurses him back to health.

Of course, the lonely Penny and beautiful Catherine fall in love, and Penny begins to develop fatherly feelings toward Horace. And the old cowboy considers settling down and experiencing the life he never had. For a while it seems like the arrangement—a family—could work, but eventually Penny departs, never to return.

❊ BEST OF THE REAL ❊

WILD WEST

BY KEN AMOROSANO FOR *AMERICAN COWBOY* MAGAZINE

The gunfighter era of the Old West spawned a number of deadly shootists, drawn from the ranks of lawmen, cowboys, ranchers, gamblers, and, of course, outlaws. We asked a group of panelists to rank the gunfighters they deemed the Old West's greatest.

10. Harry Wheeler, a captain of the Arizona Rangers and longtime sheriff, was an expert with pistol or rifle.

9. Texas Ranger Captain John Reynolds Hughes hunted down murderers, smugglers, and rustlers along the Rio Grande.

8. Dallas Stoudenmire was credited for reducing crime in El Paso at the end of a gun.

7. Harvey Logan, also known as Kid Curry, ran with Butch Cassidy and the Sundance Kid's infamous Wild Bunch gang.

6. The Shootout at the OK Corral is America's most famous gunfight and the biggest single reason for Wyatt Earp's celebrity as a gunfighter.

5. In more than a dozen gunfights, Ben Thompson killed four and wounded several others. He lived by the gun, gambling, and drink. Could be the perfect gentleman or a vicious killer.

4. One of the longest-lived of the gunfighters, John Selman killed a half-dozen men in eight gunfights. His killing of John Wesley Hardin seems to have been little more than an execution.

3. During the last four years of his life, Billy the Kid engaged in sixteen shootouts, killing four and helping kill five others.

2. John Wesley Hardin arguably killed more men than any other.

1. James Butler "Wild Bill" Hickok, known as the Prince of Pistoleers, was said to have killed seven men in as many gunfights.

The Treasure of the Sierra Madre

1948; directed by John Huston; written by John Huston and based on the novel by B. Traven; starring Humphrey Bogart and Walter Huston

Set in 1920s Mexico, *The Treasure of the Sierra Madre* is one of the greatest adventure movies ever made, one of John Huston's best films, and a fabulous Humphrey Bogart outing.

Two Americans, down on their luck, find themselves in Mexico, where they meet up with a grizzled prospector and decide to take their chances searching for gold. Their difficulties lie in the fact that as foreigners the men are potentially subject to being arrested by the Federales, or the new Federal Police in post-revolution Mexico; murdered by bandits—a serious problem in that time and in that place; or done in by their own greed when they eventually do find the gold.

A tremendous adventure story based on the great tradition of the get-rich-quick scheme, it is also the source of one of the most famous original lines in movie history. Often misquoted as "We don't need no stinking badges!," the line actually is (in response to Humphrey Bogart asking a federale, "If you're the police, where are your badges?") "Badges? We ain't got no badges. We don't need no badges! I don't have to show you any stinkin' badges!"

John Huston won Academy Awards for directing and for writing (adapted screenplay). Walter Huston, John Huston's father, also won the Academy Award for Best Supporting Actor for his role as the curmudgeonly gold miner, the first father-son win. The film was nominated for Best Picture. In 1990, this film was among the first one hundred movies selected for preservation in the United States National Film Registry by the Library of Congress as being "culturally, historically, or aesthetically significant."

———•—•———

The Treasure of the Sierra Madre was one of the first Hollywood films to be filmed almost entirely on location outside the United States (in the state of Durango and street scenes in Tampico, Mexico), although the night scenes were filmed back in the studio.

———•—•———

Humphrey Bogart and Tim Holt, *The Treasure of the Sierra Madre*, Warner Brothers, 1948 MPTVIMAGES.COM

Butch Cassidy and the Sundance Kid

1969; directed by George Roy Hill; written by William Goldman; starring Paul Newman and Robert Redford

Released the same year as the violent, bloody, and controversial *The Wild Bunch, Butch Cassidy and the Sundance Kid,* with its famous outlaws-on-a-bicycle scene, was a refreshing, entertaining, light-hearted movie that remains a favorite with audiences to this day.

Based on the true story of and myths about the real Butch Cassidy and the Sundance Kid, the movie focuses on the friendship and camaraderie shared by the two legendary outlaws. Portrayed in the movie as Robin Hoodesque characters, their exploits set them as gentle antiheroes only interested in mocking authority and defying the establishment. But after their run from the law leads them to a cliff in Bolivia, the Thelma-and-Louise style leap into the unknown only solidified their myth and their place in the story of the West. Though we suppose that Thelma and Louise really made a Butch-and-Sundance-style leap into the Grand Canyon.

The screenplay by William Goldman features humorous dialogue and slapstick comedy—along with the traditional Western action. It is one of the highest-grossing Westerns ever made and of its seven Academy Award nominations, it won four Oscars: Goldman for Best Story and Best Screenplay, Conrad Hall for cinematography, and Burt Bacharach for Best Song ("Raindrops Keep Falling on My Head," lyrics by Hal David) and Best Original Score.

———•·•———

Paul Newman and Robert Redford would co-star together once more in 1973 in George Roy Hill's Best Picture winner *The Sting.*

———•·•———

Paul Newman, *Butch Cassidy and the Sundance Kid,* © 1969, 20th Century Fox MPTV

The Ox-Bow Incident

1943; directed by William A. Wellman; written by Lamar Trotti, based on the novel by Walter Van Tilburg Clark; starring Henry Fonda, Dana Andrews, Anthony Quinn

Vigilante justice—or whether vigilantism is justice—is the theme of this grim, low-budget masterpiece based on the novel by Walter Van Tilburg Clark. Just as two drifters pass through a small Western town, news comes that a rancher has been murdered for his cattle. The townsfolk and the drifters form a posse and find the men in possession of the cattle and prepare the noose without a trial. As the movie unfolds it becomes an authoritative indictment of angry mob rule and violence.

Henry Fonda was named the star of the movie, but this is ensemble acting at its best—and Fonda both worked for scale and helped raise money to fund the movie in the first place. The movie was actually completed two years before it was released in theaters, which were mostly running morale-boosting, feel-good movies during the war years. And it didn't do well at the box office when it was released, although it was nominated for Best Picture at the Academy Awards.

Henry Fonda and Harry Morgan, *The Ox-Bow Incident*, Twentieth Century Fox, 1943 MPTVIMAGES.COM

The Man Who Shot Liberty Valance

1962; directed by John Ford; written by James Warner Bellah and Willis Goldbeck, based on the story by Dorothy M. Johnson; starring John Wayne, James Stewart, and Vera Miles

In the late nineteenth century, U.S. Senator Ransom Stoddard (James Stewart) and his wife (Vera Miles) have returned to the small Western town of Shinbone in order to attend the funeral of Tom Doniphon. A newspaper editor asks the senator to explain why he has come to bury an apparent nobody and the film unfolds in flashback.

As it turns out, Rance Stoddard's entire political career, from his days as the territorial representative through his current senatorial stint, has been based on the general belief that he was the "man who shot Liberty Valance," a much-feared outlaw who terrorized the town of Shinbone while working for the cattle barons who opposed statehood. Stoddard himself believed the story at first and was hesitant, as a killer, to take a post in Washington. But as it turns out, Tom Doniphon was standing in the shadows during the fateful shootout between Stoddard and Valance and was actually responsible for firing the shot that got Stoddard credit for a heroic deed—in such a way that he'd probably be put on trial for murder if it was known. Doniphon did it for the love of his life, Vera, and Vera ended up with Stoddard anyway.

After Doniphon's death, Stoddard finally confesses the whole story to the editor of the newspaper. But, of course, he refuses to publish it and burns the notes of the interview, saying, "This is the West, sir. When the legend becomes fact, print the legend."

A fitting epigraph for a lot of the Westerns on this list.

———•·•———

The Burt Bacharach and Hal David song "The Man Who Shot Liberty Valance," which became a Top 10 Hit for Gene Pitney, wasn't recorded until after the movie came out.

———•·•———

Monte Walsh

1970; directed by William A. Fraker; written by David Zelag Goodman and Lukas Heller; starring Lee Marvin, Jeanne Moreau, and Jack Palance

A lot of Western movies made in the late 1960s and early 1970s seemed to hone in on the "end of the West" or the end of the Wild West and the rapid encroachment of civilization, railroads, and barbed wire. In this fairly obscure 1970 movie—obscure at least until the 2008 TV remake starring Tom Selleck—Lee Marvin plays Monte Walsh, the aging cowboy trying to deal with the changes that would come with the end of the Wild West era.

Lee Marvin's performance makes this movie. There are tender scenes between him and his prostitute girlfriend, played by Jeanne Moreau, and Jack Palance brings his usual understated presence to the movie as well. Eventually, the cowboys realize that their age and the changes that have come are insurmountable obstacles to keeping the way of life they once had and they have to find a way to move on.

———•———

The theme song for *Monte Walsh* was sung by Mama Cass Elliot of the Mamas and the Papas.

———•———

Broken Arrow

1950; directed by Delmer Daves; written by Albert Maltz (Michael Blankfort) and based on the novel by Elliott Arnold; starring James Stewart, Jeff Chandler, and Debra Paget

The first Western made after World War II that took a sensitive and sympathetic view of Native Americans, *Broken Arrow* dramatizes the true story of the unusual relationship between Tom Jeffords (played by Jimmy Stewart) and Cochise (Jeff Chandler), the Apache chief in 1860s Arizona Territory.

While it is true that Jeffords's act of bravery in riding to the rescue of white mail couriers held by the Apache led to the understanding between the two men, and it is also true that this film was groundbreaking in its attempts to show both sides of the story, this is a Hollywood movie, embroidered for the viewing audience. The character of Sonsenbray (Debra Paget) was created as a love interest for Jeffords. They are married, but their romance ends tragically when she's killed by whites in an ambush. True to the film's message, the plot then revolves around her not dying in vain—and showing the Native Americans as humans, not as savages hostile to settlers for no good reason.

The film was nominated for three Academy Awards and won a Golden Globe award for Best Film Promoting International Understanding.

———•·•———

"The Apache Wedding Prayer," still a popular reading at weddings of all kinds to this day, was written for this movie.

———•·•———

My Darling Clementine

1946; directed by John Ford; written by Samuel G. Engel, Winston Miller, and Sam Hellman, based on the book *Wyatt Earp, Frontier Marshal* by Stuart N. Lake; starring Henry Fonda, Linda Darnell, and Victor Mature

There's a great scene in the TV series *M*A*S*H* when Colonel Potter (Harry Morgan) brings in this classic John Ford epic for the docs and troops to watch in the mess tent one night—and they get as far as Henry Fonda rolling onto the screen and growling out a few terse lines before mayhem ensues. For anyone who's only seen that clip, this movie is well worth a peek past the first thirty seconds.

Fonda, the terrific character actor, plays the legendary marshal, Wyatt Earp, in the raw and open days of Tombstone just before the legendary shootout at the O.K. Corral. John Ford chose Monument Valley in northern Arizona as the setting for the movie and named it for the civilizing female acquaintance of Earp in Tombstone at the time. And Ford chooses to, amid the fabrications around the true story of Earp and the O.K. Corral, spin a legend of a feud between the good Earps and the wicked Clantons that comes to a violent head, the Earps representing the good civilizing forces coming to the West and the Clantons, the evil that needs to be eradicated.

Henry Fonda, *My Darling Clementine*, © 1946, Twentieth Century Fox MPTVIMAGES.COM

WYATT EARP

LAWMAN OF THE SILVER SCREEN

By the time *My Darling Clementine* was released in 1946, movies based on the story of the shoot-out at the O.K. Corral and Wyatt Earp had already been made many times earlier:

Law and Order (1932) with Walter Huston as the Earp-like character

Frontier Marshal (1934) with George O'Brien as Earp

Frontier Marshal (1939) with Randolph Scott as Wyatt Earp and Cesar Romero as John "Doc" Holliday

Tombstone: The Town Too Tough to Die (1942) with Richard Dix

And more would come later:

Gunfight at O.K. Corral (1957) with Burt Lancaster as Earp and Kirk Douglas as Holliday

Hour of the Gun (1967) with James Garner as Earp and Jason Robards Jr. as Holliday

Doc (1971) with Harris Yulin as Earp and Stacy Keach as Holliday

Tombstone (1993) with Kurt Russell as Earp and Val Kilmer as Holliday

Wyatt Earp (1994) with Kevin Costner as Earp and Dennis Quaid as Holliday

Lonely Are the Brave

1962; directed by David Miller; written by Dalton Trumbo, based on the novel *The Brave Cowboy* by Edward Abbey; starring Kirk Douglas, Gena Rowlands, and Walter Matthau

The days of the Old West are basically over, but John W. "Jack" Burns (Kirk Douglas) still scrapes a living as a roaming cowboy, refusing to give up the life he loves to the point of sticking to his fiercely independent guns, refusing to get any kind of official identification. The wife of an old friend, Jerry Bondi (played by Gena Rowlands) tracks him down to ask for help for her husband Paul, who is in jail for aiding illegal immigrants.

Jack tries to get arrested by starting a violent barroom brawl against a one-armed man and succeeds after he punches the arresting officer. His goal is to be jailed with Paul and to persuade him to escape, feeling that it's not right for him to be punished.

Of course, Paul Bondi refuses to break out, so Jack goes on his own and is the pursued by the sympathetic sheriff (Walter Matthau) and the sadistic deputy who has already assaulted him while in jail. In the end, Jack and his horse end up on a collision course with a tractor-trailer when they try to cross a busy highway.

Kirk Douglas was nominated for a 1963 BAFTA Award as Best Foreign Actor for his work in *Lonely Are the Brave,* and placed third in the Laurel Awards for Top Action Performance.

———•·•———

This is one of the first film appearances of Carroll O'Connor (Archie Bunker)—he's the driver of the semi.

———•·•———

Rancho Notorious

1952; directed by Fritz Lang; written by Daniel Taradash and based on a story by Silvia Richards; starring Marlene Dietrich, Arthur Kennedy, and Mel Ferrer

Marlene Dietrich is, of course, such a legend of the motion picture Western that she was given her very own spoof by the fabulously talented Madeleine Kahn in the great parody of Westerns, *Blazing Saddles*. And *Rancho Notorious* is one of her greatest roles—she plays Altar Keane, the boss of Chuck-a-Luck, the criminal hideout where Vern Haskell, a nice rancher, ends up when he sets out to avenge the death of his fiancée at the hands of a vicious bandit.

Based on the story "Gunsight Whitman" by Silvia Richards, this tale of revenge takes many twists and turns as Vern tracks the outlaw responsible for his beloved's death to Chuck-a-Luck, figures out his identity when Marlene Dietrich appears wearing the jeweled brooch he'd given to his fiancée, and then kills him in a shootout. But the path to that shootout is worth the viewing.

Fort Apache

1948; directed by John Ford; written by Frank S. Nugent and James Warner Bellah; starring John Wayne, Henry Fonda, and Shirley Temple

JOHN FORD CAVALRY TRILOGY

Owen Thursday (Henry Fonda) sees his posting to the desolate Fort Apache after the Civil War as a chance for military honor; the men stationed there see him as an arrogant and egotistical officer and recognize his lack of experience with the Native Americans he's expected to handle. They all thought that Captain Kirby York (John Wayne) should have taken command.

The arrogant Thursday ignores York's advice about treating the Apache with respect, refuses to allow his daughter Philadelphia (Shirley Temple) to court one of the soldiers, and eventually, disastrously attempts to destroy the Apache chief Cochise in a battle that nearly wipes out Thursday's entire command.

John Wayne, John Agar, Shirley Temple, and Henry Fonda, *Fort Apache,* **RKO, 1948** COURTESY OF THE ACADEMY OF MOTION PICTURE ARTS AND SCIENCES

She Wore a Yellow Ribbon

1949; directed by John Ford; written by James Warner Bellah, Frank S. Nugent, and Laurence Stallings; starring John Wayne, Joanne Dru, Ben Johnson, and John Agar

JOHN FORD CAVALRY TRILOGY

Of the three films in this group, *She Wore a Yellow Ribbon* is, appropriately perhaps, the only one that was produced in color. The budget of $1.6 million made it one of the most expensive Westerns made to date, but it was a major hit that remains popular today.

Filmed, as *Fort Apache* was, in Monument Valley on the Navajo reservation in Arizona, the movie is named for a common U.S. military song, "She Wore a Yellow Ribbon," which is used to keep marching cadence. In the movie, the aging U.S. Cavalry Capt. Nathan Cutting Brittles (John Wayne) sets out on one last patrol to deal with a band of Cheyenne and Arapaho who have left their reservation after Custer's defeat at Little Big Horn. With him are the wife and niece of the commanding officer, whom he is to deliver to an East-bound stage. And his charge is to deal with the flight of the Native Americans while avoiding a new Indian war.

———•·•———

The film's narrator says that Pony Express riders were reporting George Custer's defeat at the Battle of the Little Bighorn, but Custer was killed in 1876, fifteen years after the Pony Express ended service.

———•·•———

Rio Grande

1950; directed by John Ford; written by James Kevin McGuinness and based on a story by James Warner Bellah; starring John Wayne and Maureen O'Hara

JOHN FORD CAVALRY TRILOGY

John Wayne also stars in this third film in Ford's cavalry trilogy, this time as Lieutenant Colonel Kirby York, now in charge of the outpost on the Rio Grande where he's training troops as part of the Army's post–Civil War efforts to "tame" the Apaches and other tribes on the Western frontier. His estranged son, who he hasn't seen for fifteen years, turns up as one of the trainees—and then his estranged wife (Maureen O'Hara) shows up to talk her son out of serving. In the end, York fights to save his honor and to put his family back together.

Ford wanted to make the great Wayne/O'Hara vehicle *The Quiet Man* before *Rio Grande*, but the studio head insisted that he do *Rio Grande* first to pay for later film, since he didn't think it would perform as well at the box office as the Western. Of course, when it was released in 1952, *The Quiet Man* would become Republic's number one money-making film.

The Gunfighter

1950; directed by Henry King; written by William Bowers, William Sellers, and Andre DeToth; starring Gregory Peck and Helen Westcott

The notorious gunfighter Jimmy Ringo (Gregory Peck) has a reputation for being the fastest draw in the West—a fact that leads to nothing but trouble. Challenged by a young man named Eddie, Ringo kills him and is then pursued by his three brothers, who are seeking revenge.

After he escapes his pursuers, Ringo heads to a nearby town where he hopes to see his estranged wife and young son and convince them that he's reformed and wants to head to California to start a new life together. In the end, however, Ringo is killed by someone else who wants revenge for a killing (though it turns out Ringo wasn't responsible) before he can live up to his wife's expectations—but he takes the blame for the shootout with his dying breath rather than doom someone else to a life of being challenged for being the fastest draw in the West. And in the tearjerking scene at the end, he finally gets his wife's forgiveness.

Rio Bravo

1959; directed by Howard Hawks; written by Jules Futhman and Leigh Bracket, based on the story by B. H. McCampbell; starring John Wayne, Dean Martin, and Ricky Nelson

One of Howard Hawks's best films, *Rio Bravo* relates the tale of a small-town sheriff forced to recruit a rag-tag group of misfits to keep order in town as he holds the brother of a local villain in jail. By no means a musical, with Dean Martin and Ricky Nelson in the cast, songs were still called for, and three featured in the soundtrack: "My Rifle, My Pony, and Me," "Get Along Home, Cindy," and "Rio Bravo."

The story follows the fairly conventional themes of traditional Westerns—gunfights, fistfights, and ranching interests vs. town interests. Many film historians believe that this movie was made as a response to the allegory of Hollywood blacklisting that was *High Noon.* Rather than being a lone man against the world, John T. Chance, as played by Wayne, is surrounded by allies—the whole town rallies at the end to support him and his deputies.

Winchester '73

1950; directed by Anthony Mann; written by Robert L. Richards, Borden Chase, and Stuart N. Lake; starring James Stewart and Shelley Winters

A prized Winchester '73 rifle is the protagonist in this Jimmy Stewart/Anthony Mann production, the first of five Westerns that the actor and director would make together. Lin McAdam (Jimmy Stewart) wins the rifle in a marksmanship contest; the loser of the contest, Dutch Henry Brown (Stephen McNally), steals it almost immediately; and then Lin McAdam tracks it across the country until he recovers it in a final showdown.

Shelley Winters is terrific as the dancehall girl, Lola, forced out of Dodge City by the Earp brothers. She gets caught up in the chase for the rifle, a battle with Indians, and the other plot twists and turns as the gun changes hands through card games, murder, trickery, and deceit to the end of the movie—where Lin McAdam and the rifle are reunited and Lin gets the girl.

———————

After the deaths of her husband and young child, the heir to the Winchester rifle fortune, Mrs. Sarah Winchester, fled to California in the 1890s claiming spirits had sent her there to atone for the thousands of deaths caused by the guns that "won the West." Her "assignment" was to build a home for all the spirits—if she stopped her progress, she would die. She started with a small farmhouse and added onto it and remodeled it for thirty-four years before succumbing to old age.

———————

James Stewart, *Winchester '73*, Universal Pictures, 1950

John Wayne, *Hondo*, Warner Brothers, 1953, © 1978 Bud Fraker MPTVIMAGES.COM

Hondo

1953; directed by John Farrow; written by James Edward Grant, based on the short story "The Gift of Cochise" by Louis L'Amour; starring John Wayne and Geraldine Page

Homesteader Angie Lowe (Geraldine Page) and her nine-year-old son Johnny (Lee Aker) are eking out a living on a remote ranch in the New Mexico desert when they spot a stranger with a saddle and rifle, but no horse, drinking from the stream on their property. The stranger, Hondo Lane (John Wayne) says he is a U.S. Army scout, part Apache, whose horse had been stolen a few days earlier. Lane offers Angie military scrip and chores in exchange for a new horse, realizing that her husband has been gone for some time.

Eventually, Angie realizes that the man is not what he seems, and she kicks him off her property. Naturally, in spite of previously good relations, Angie and Johnny are attacked by Apaches shortly after he leaves the ranch.

Later, Hondo makes his way back to the ranch and into Angie's arms (after killing her errant husband during an earlier gunfight), the army gets involved, and there is a battle with the Apaches that marks what Hondo says is the end of their way of life.

John Wayne's production company Batjac partnered with Warner Brothers to make the movie, which was shot in the "new" 3-D technology on location in Mexico—a very difficult process due to the technology of the time. It was less gimmicky than many 3-D movies, but showed the depth of the desert landscape rather than objects flying at the camera. Unfortunately, that wave of the 3-D fad had already started to wane when the movie was released, but it was still very popular with audiences and with or without the 3-D effects is a classic of the Wayne oeuvre.

THE MAKING OF AN ICON

BY RAYMOND E. WHITE FOR *AMERICAN COWBOY*

Seventy years after his first starring roll in a Western, *The Big Trail* (1930), John Wayne remains the nation's most cherished cultural hero. His hold on the public is as strong today as it was at the time of his death in 1979. No twenty-first-century American celebrity shows any sign of challenging his preeminence. Wayne's body of work gets more airplay than any other star's and retail chains such as Wal-Mart and Target sell more videos of his films than any other performer's. As if to further cement his stature, in 2000 American Movie Classics declared Wednesday to be John Wayne Day. Not just a particular Wednesday. *Every Wednesday.*

Robert Osborne, the on-air host for Turner Classic Movies, told *American Cowboy* that there's been no slackening in public demand for John Wayne films.

"I think he has reached icon status now," Osborne said of Wayne. "It's no longer like he was someone who really lived—it's like he's part of American folklore. John Wayne, now more than anybody, seems to embody those rugged individualist traits that people would like to have in themselves. Everybody would like to be as commanding and confident as he was, and there was also a humanity about him. We liked him. And not just people from his era. Kids today know John Wayne."

Osborne said he met Wayne on more than one occasion, including a time when he (Osborne) was only in his twenties. He attended a birthday party for Wayne's son Pat, and was impressed when the big guy made it a point to greet each guest individually.

"He wasn't being a movie star—he was just being a good dad," Osborne said. "During the course of the evening he came around and said, 'Hi, I'm John Wayne,' and said it as though we wouldn't have known who he was. Nothing presumptuous about it. And like a good dad, he just disappeared then. He was a really nice guy."

Osborne said that though it's the older Wayne with whom viewers are most familiar, the younger Wayne was already well on his way to defining what the older Wayne was all about.

"When you're used to seeing the older Wayne, it's incredible to see him as a kid—to see how fresh-faced and attractive and likeable he was. He kept that as time went on. I still see that same lanky guy [in John Wayne's earlier films], with that walk and that smile. I think he was a better actor than he got credit for being. Those who criticize him never got in front of a camera. He made it look so easy. People didn't think he did any work, but it was more work than anyone believed."

For his own part, Wayne maintained that he was not an actor. "I don't act—I react," he often said. Why he offered this denial remains a puzzle, because Wayne labored tirelessly at his trade. It was in the 1930s that he began to mold the image that would make him a national institution.

The important thing for Wayne was to be natural and comfortable in the role. Working in nearly seventy films in the '30s, he had ample opportunity to experiment. Having been an athlete and, later, a stunt man, he seemed most at ease in action scenes. But Wayne applied himself to dialogue, and as the voice and the mannerisms emerged, these traits, combined with the physical presence, projected an image of simplicity, straightforwardness, and consistency. In those early Westerns, he usually portrayed an independent, self-assured, take-charge hero.

Never flashy or flamboyant in his appearance, Wayne disdained immaculate white suits or fringed and flower-patterned shirts. He dressed modestly in jeans, boots, a simple Western shirt, a kerchief, the obligatory big hat, and sometimes a vest. Usually he packed a single revolver, belted and holstered low on his hips. We see him ending the decade of the '30s in pretty much the same attire as he started it. Indeed, this style—and Wayne's resistance to the showier wardrobe styles of the Gene Autrys and Roy Rogerses of that era—probably helped him to make the transition to big-budget films in the 1940s and helped him to survive the fates of a whole posse of B-Western bravos. His was an emphasis on the inward man rather than the outward appearance. We see it carried on in the great pictures he made in the following decades—in *Angel and the Badman* (1947), *Hondo* (1953), *The Man Who Shot Liberty Valance* (1962), *El Dorado* (1967), and in even his character role as Rooster Cogburn in *True Grit* (1969).

If there was any significant change in the character through the '30s, it was an ever-more-tangible psychological depth. We see it especially in the classic *Stagecoach* (1939), in which Wayne as the Ringo Kid balances the burden of a dark past with the positivism that audiences had already come to expect of him. It would be an unfolding theme for the rising star, and would culminate in his classic films under director John Ford in the 1950s, when the Western, and Wayne, struck their highest cinematic notes.

In the '30s, Wayne was still formulating that persona, but even in those simple stories it is clear that the actor is striving to express certain ideals and values. In some cases he did so through action; in others, it may have been a word, a look, or even his crooked smile.

It must have been easy for those Depression-era moviegoers to sit in a dark theater and project their own selves, as well as to unburden their own troubles, onto this handsome, virile cowboy hero who seemed to sum up what they thought of as the best in themselves and their fellow man. In his later films, whether they were war movies or Westerns, Wayne went on connecting with audiences in the same way. He may not have recognized himself as an actor, but his ability to strike such chords in the hearts of millions of Americans makes him a litmus in our understanding of ourselves, then and now. As we plunge deeper into this uncertain century, he still stands as a reminder of who we were, and, for many, his was a way that could see us, as a people, through many troubles and adversities yet to come.

The Man from Laramie

1955; directed by Anthony Mann; written by Philip Yordan, Frank Burt, and based on a story by Thomas T. Flynn; starring James Stewart, Arthur Kennedy, and Donald Crisp

The collaborations of James Stewart and Anthony Mann just work, as evidenced by this family drama that plays out in Coronado, an isolated western town where Will Lockhart (James Stewart) becomes entangled in the drama after delivering supplies there and looking for information about who has been selling guns to the local Apaches, who killed his brother.

The Waggomans are the royal family of Coronado, headed by patriarch Alec Waggoman (Donald Crisp) and put on a track to destruction by his arrogant son Dave Waggoman (Alex Nicol). Lockhart ends up on a collision course with the Waggomans after he's told by a niece of Alec's, Barbara Waggoman, that he can collect salt and haul it away, but when Dave finds out he accuses Lockhart of stealing, shoots his mules, and burns his wagons. Later it turns out that Dave is behind the gun sale to the Apaches.

The ending of this movie has the flavor of a Shakespearean tragedy and a surprise for the viewer.

Ulzana's Raid

1972; directed by Robert Aldrich; written by Alan Sharp; starring Burt Lancaster, Bruce Davison, and Joaquin Martinez

In this bleak 1972 movie about the Indian wars that followed the Civil War, Ulzana is the ultimate antihero. The sympathetic Apache leader who flees his reservation with a band of followers is intent on revenging his people against the white man. In this, one of the best of the revisionist Westerns and an allegory on the Vietnam War, we see the Native Americans as the victims, fighting to save their culture from the encroaching and greedy whites, but the Apache are also give their due as much better fighters because of their familiarity with the land.

Report reaches the U.S. Cavalry that the Apache leader Ulzana has left his reservation with a band of followers. A compassionate young officer, Lieutenant DeBuin, is given a small company to find him and bring him back; accompanying the troops is McIntosh, an experienced scout, and Ke-Ni-Tay, an Apache guide. Ulzana massacres, rapes, and loots across the countryside; and as DeBuin encounters the remains of his victims, he is compelled to learn from McIntosh and to confront his own naïveté and hidden prejudices.

Eventually, the cavalry catches up with Ulzana—and a battle ensues. The movie's end sees Lieutenant DeBuin leading the few survivors back to the fort.

Blood on the Moon

1948; directed by Robert Wise; written by Lillie Hayward, based on the novel by Luke Short; starring Robert Mitchum, Barbara Bel Geddes, and Walter Brennan

Robert Wise's *Blood on the Moon* is as much psychological thriller as it is Western. And it succeeds handily on both fronts by abandoning the formulaic aspects of either. One of the biggest reasons for its success is the way Robert Mitchum embodies the character of the shady-looking stranger who's ridden into town to go to work for his old friend. As written by Lillie Hayward, his character is honest but interesting. When Jim Garry (Mitchum) realizes that his old friend is in fact a swindler set on destroying the homesteaders' livelihoods, the two become sworn enemies and the drama starts.

At the end, of course, there's a bloody showdown, but the journey is where the interest lies in this post–World War II cowboy movie that's more than a cowboy movie.

Major Dundee

1965; directed by Sam Peckinpah; written by Harry Julian Fink, Oscar Saul, and Sam Peckinpah; starring Charlton Heston, Richard Harris, and James Coburn

Major Dundee is a violent (by 1960s standards), fascinating character study directed by Sam Peckinpah. Based on real historical events in the last year of the Civil War (though the events are drawn from far-distant locations and loosely interpreted), the story focuses on Union cavalry officer Major Amos Dundee (Charlton Heston) who is sent to New Mexico territory to head a prisoner-of-war camp after he's relieved of his regular command.

Many critics compare the story and the action as it unfolds to *Moby-Dick,* with Dundee as Ahab and the young soldier narrating as Ishmael. Actor R. G. Armstrong, who plays a small role in the film, even called it *"Moby-Dick* on horseback." The Apache, and their leader, Charriba, stand in for the legendary white whale and Dundee's twin obsessions—glory for himself and hunting down the "savages"—underline the comparisons to Ahab; though in the end Charriba

and his band are defeated, the costs to the men around Dundee are severe.

Major Dundee made Peckinpah's image as a renegade filmmaker, but problems with the production of the movie led to a hasty first theatrical release that was a box-office failure. Charlton Heston alleged that toward the end of shooting the movie, Peckinpah would become drunk and wander off, and Heston would step in to direct. Still, as a character study this one stands out—and has stood the test of time.

Peckinpah was supposedly so abusive to the cast and crew when drunk on the set—evidently a regular occurrence—that Charlton Heston had to threaten him with a cavalry saber.

Charlton Heston and Richard Harris, *Major Dundee,* 1965, Columbia © 1978 Mel Traxel MPTVIMAGES.COM

The Magnificent Seven

1960; directed by John Sturges; written by William Roberts; starring Steve McQueen, Charles Bronson, Eli Wallach, and Yul Brynner

The Magnificent Seven is, of course, a remake of the classic Kurosawa film, *Seven Samurai,* but it has become a classic in its own right, earning a spot in the top fifty on our list easily.

The great Eli Wallach plays Calvera, a bandit who routinely raids a small village with his band of thugs, and finally the town decides to take a stand, pleading with a gunfighter named Chris (Yul Brynner) who eventually agrees to try to help them fight Calvera, managing to recruit six men to help. In addition to Brynner and Wallach, the remarkable cast includes Steve McQueen, Charles Bronson, James Coburn, Robert Vaughn, Horst Buchholz, and Brad Dexter. The seven men band together and train the residents to fight, bonding with them in the process but eventually betrayal, disloyalty, and distrust color the relationships and lead to tragic consequences.

Eventually, of course, the gunfighters take a stand against the bandits, though their losses are severe. In the end, Chris rides away remarking, "Only the farmers won. We lost. We always lose."

Eli Wallach, Charles Bronson, Brad Dexter, Horst Buchholz, Yul Brynner, Steve McQueen, Robert Vaughn, and James Coburn, *The Magnificent Seven*, United Artists, 1960 MPTVIMAGES.COM

The Naked Spur

1953; directed by Anthony Mann; written by Sam Rolfe and Harold Jack Bloom; starring James Stewart, Janet Leigh, and Robert Ryan

Ben Vandergroat (Robert Ryan) is wanted for the murder of a marshal in Abilene, Kansas, and Howard Kemp (James Stewart) is tracking him through the Rocky Mountains of Colorado, where he hires a grizzled old prospector to help him search and then recruits a Union soldier (this is 1868) who's been dishonorably discharged from the Army and is retreating from his post in Bozeman, Montana Territory.

Eventually, the trio catches up with Vandergroat and his companion, Lina Patch (Janet Leigh), and it's revealed that Kemp is out for the $5,000 reward for the capture of Vandergroat. The psychological warfare sets in as the outlaw tries to turn the bounty hunters against each other through their greed and by using his beautiful companion to set off jealous impulses as they try to take him back to Kansas to receive the bounty on his head.

Everyone in the group has a secret, and those secrets and fighting loyalties make for a riveting journey back to "civilization" or wherever the road and their pasts take them.

❧ SPAGHETTI WESTERNS ❧

In the twenty-first century the so-called "Spaghetti" Western has become so much a part of the American Western movie tradition that it's hard to imagine a time when *The Good the Bad and the Ugly* was not a part of our cultural conscience. But when they were first produced in the late 1950s and early 1960s, the movies—filmed entirely in Italian in landscapes that mimicked the American West and initially released in Italian—were largely discounted by critics and audiences. Now, of course, the minimalist style of work like Sergio Leone's and the scores of composer Ennio Morricone have made The Dollars Trilogy and *Once Upon a Time in the West* not only great examples of the subgenre but movies that fall squarely in a list of 100 of the Greatest Westerns of All Time.

After the release of *Il Terrore dell'Oklahoma* in 1959, the 1960s and 1970s were the greatest period of production for Spaghetti Westerns. Here are a few others not included in our top 100 but still worth checking out:

Savage Guns, 1961
Treasure of Silver Lake, 1962
Gunfight at Red Sands, 1963
Ride and Kill, 1964
Minnesota Clay, 1965
A Pistol for Ringo, 1965
Viva Maria, 1965
Navajo Joe, 1966
Django, 1966
Any Gun Can Play, 1967
The Great Silence, 1968
Trinity Is Still My Name, 1971
A Fistful of Dynamite, 1971
My Name Is Nobody, 1973
Keoma, 1976

A Fistful of Dollars

1964; directed by Sergio Leone; written by A. Bonzzoni and Víctor Andrés Catena; starring Clint Eastwood and Marianne Koch

SERGIO LEONE DOLLARS TRILOGY

First released in Italy in 1964, and then in the United States in 1967, *A Fistful of Dollars,* the first of the "Dollars trilogy," ushered in the era of popular spaghetti Westerns, but it was itself an unofficial remake of a 1961 Japanese film, *Yojimbo,* directed by Akira Kurosawa, which was in turn influenced by early American Westerns.

Thus, through many twirls around the pasta fork, we arrive at Clint Eastwood, "the Man with No Name" who saunters into the little Mexican border town of San Miguel where a bitter feud between two families is simmering. The Man with No Name sees an opportunity and decides to play the families against each other in order to make a little money when Mexican soldiers come through town with a load of gold to trade with American troops for weapons. After the drama comes to a head, he leaves town as mysteriously as he arrives.

Sergio Leone wanted to reinvent the Western genre in Italy and reinvigorate what he thought was stagnant filmmaking in America in the 1950s. With this and with the next two Dollars movies, he managed to breathe new life into the genre and created Italian and American icons.

A Fistful of Dollars was an Italian/German/Spanish co-production and there was a significant language barrier on the set. Leone did not speak English, and Eastwood didn't speak Italian and communicated with the Italian cast and crew mostly through stuntman Benito Stefanelli.

Clint Eastwood and Margarita Lozano, *A Fistful of Dollars*, Director Sergio Leone, Ocean Films, 1964

For a Few Dollars More

1965; directed by Sergio Leone; written by Sergio Leone and Fulvio Morsella; starring Clint Eastwood and Lee Van Cleef

SERGIO LEONE DOLLARS TRILOGY

The premise of the next movie in the Dollars trilogy is pretty straightforward. Clint Eastwood (the Man with No Name) and Lee Van Cleef (the Man in Black) are two bounty hunters separately in pursuit of the notorious fugitive El Indio (Gian Maria Volonté) and his gang. Eventually, the two bounty hunters learn about each other and decide to team up to take down Indio and his gang.

Indio robs a bank in El Paso and takes the money to the small border town of Agua Caliente where the bounty hunters catch up with him and the reasons for their pursuit are revealed.

One of the great things about all three of these films are the scores by Ennio Morricone. It's almost another character—and Sergio Leone would actually film scenes with it playing.

Lee Van Cleef and Gian Maria Volonte, *For a Few Dollars More,* United Artists, 1965 MPTVIMAGES.COM

The Good, the Bad, and the Ugly

1966; directed by Sergio Leone; written by Luciano Vincenzoni and Sergio Leone; starring Clint Eastwood, Lee Van Cleef, and Eli Wallach

SERGIO LEONE DOLLARS TRILOGY

The plot of the violent, thrilling third movie in the Dollars trilogy revolves around three gunslingers all competing to find the same fortune in buried Confederate gold in a cemetery. One knows the name of the cemetery, one knows the name on the grave where it's buried, and the third is a ruthless mercenary bent on torturing the information out of them.

Clint Eastwood plays Blondie, aka The Good, aka the Man with No Name. Lee Van Cleef is Angel Eyes: The Bad, a ruthless, unfeeling and sociopathic villain. And Eli Wallach is Tuco Benedicto Pacífico Juan María Ramírez, The Ugly, a comical, oafish (though very dangerous), fast-talking bandit who is wanted by the authorities for a long list of crimes.

When the movie first released in the United States, it was criticized for the violence, and generally looked down on as a spaghetti Western, but today it is regarded as a classic—one of the most popular and well-known movies of the genre.

———•·•———

Eli Wallach nearly died three times on the set: He was almost poisoned when he accidentally drank from a bottle of acid that a film technician had set next to his soda bottle; in the scene where he was to be hanged after a pistol was fired, the horse underneath him bolted and galloped for about a mile with Wallach's hands tied behind his back; and in the scene where Tuco has to sever a chain binding him to a henchman by laying down near a railroad track and working to get the train to run over the chain, he could easily have been decapitated by steps jutting out from the train had he moved at the wrong time.

———•·•———

Eli Wallach and Clint Eastwood, *The Good, the Bad, and the Ugly,* United Artists, 1966

Bend of the River

1952; directed by Anthony Mann; written by Borden Chase, based on the novel by William Gulick; starring Jimmy Stewart, Rock Hudson, and Harry Morgan

In this collaboration with director Anthony Mann, Jimmy Stewart plays Glyn McLyntock, a questionable character who leads a wagon train of homesteaders on the Oregon Trail from Missouri to establish a settlement outside Portland, Oregon Territory. When winter comes, McLyntock goes with one of the settlers to Portland for much needed supplies—and on their way back Emerson Cole (Arthur Kennedy), a man who McLyntock, a former outlaw himself, had rescued from being lynched for horse theft, steals the supplies so that he can sell them in a mining camp for profit—rather than taking them back to the needy settlers.

With gunfights on horseback, double-crossing former friends, and the gorgeous love interest torn between two men tempted to give in to greed, this is an epic adventure.

Tumbleweeds

1925; directed by King Baggot; written by C. Gardner Sullivan, based on the story by Hal G. Evarts; starring William S. Hart, Barbara Bedford, and Lucien Littlefield

When the cannon shot signaled the start of the Oklahoma land rush of 1893, covered wagons, surreys, stagecoaches, and wheeled vehicles of all kinds bounced across the rough prairie sod in the mad rush to claim a homestead. It was a thrilling movie moment for the audiences who went to see this 1925 silent movie that would influence later films like *Cimarron,* which won the Academy Award for Best Picture in 1931 and told a similar story.

William S. Hart, in what was probably the finest movie of his career, stars in the story of the "tumbleweed" cowboy who wants to settle down on his own place with his love, Molly. Naturally, the hero must overcome numerous obstacles in order to stake his claim and win his lady love. It was Hart's last movie. In spite of numerous offers from Hollywood producers that came in after this classic Western melodrama released in theaters, he remained retired, settling in on his ranch in California.

For today's audiences, the feat of producing the land rush with the day's technology is a novelty, but there is also something truly thrilling about the silent thundering of wheels and hooves across the prairie and the way the faces of the actors tell the story. One other remarkable thing about the movie is that the Native Americans weren't treated as villains and there were African Americans depicted as friends of the hero on screen. It was a film truly ahead of its time but rooted in it in a way that makes it both relevant and fascinating for audiences now.

Hombre

1967; directed by Martin Ritt; written by Irving Ravetch, Harriet Frank Jr., based on the novel by Elmore Leonard; starring Paul Newman, Fredric March, and Richard Boone

Set in late-nineteenth-century Arizona, the movie tells the story of a white man named John Russell (Paul Newman) who was raised by Apaches and thus shunned by "civilized" people. As the plot develops, he ends up on a stagecoach with a cross-section of Western personalities from the aristocratic and snobbish professor's wife to the proprietress of a boarding house and a couple of her boarders. When outlaws attack the stagecoach, Russell saves his fellow passengers and they ask for help in getting to safety and in rescuing the woman taken hostage, who naturally was the snobbish woman most rude to Russell.

Between Paul Newman's terse, but emotional, performance and the gorgeous writing of Elmore Leonard, *Hombre*, a groundbreaking movie in its depiction of the plight of Native Americans and American hypocrisy, is also a piece of art that's endured for more than forty years.

Hud

1963; directed by Martin Ritt; written by Irving Ravetch, based on the novel *Horseman, Pass By* by Larry McMurtry; starring Paul Newman, Patricia Neal, and Melvyn Douglas

Hud Bannon is a selfish, embittered, and ruthless modern-day cowboy in conflict with his father Homer, the ethical, principled patriarch of the Bannon clan, a Texas ranch family. Paul Newman plays Hud, who is only interested in avoiding responsibility and enjoying himself through bar brawls, driving his pink Cadillac, and having affairs with married (and unmarried) women. His nephew Lonnie (Brandon De Wilde) is caught between his admiration for his uncle and his grandfather's (Melvyn Douglas) bitterness toward Hud.

Patricia Neal plays Alma, the Bannon's housekeeper—taking a small role and turning it into an Academy Award–winning performance. After being raped by Hud, she flees the ranch, and Lonnie drives her to the bus station, discovering the injured Homer on the way home. Lonnie finally realizes the extent of Hud's depravity and abandons him after Homer dies. In the end there's no redemption or awakening for Hud, who brushes off the emptiness left to him by his own actions with a shrug.

It's in many ways a bleak story, but the beautiful interpretation of the novel by the great Larry McMurtry makes this a classic. It was nominated for seven Academy Awards, winning for Best Actress (Patricia Neal), Best Supporting Actor (Melvyn Douglas), and Best Cinematography (Black-and-White).

In the novel, *Alma*, the Bannons' black housekeeper, has a fairly significant role, but in the movie the part is a fairly small one, especially for a Best Actress–winning role.

LONESOME DOVE

BY TOM WILMES FOR *AMERICAN COWBOY*

Editor's Note: Since the scope of the one hundred best Westerns included in this book is limited to cinematic releases, we were unable to include some great made-for-TV projects—but we feel that we must pay tribute to the seminal miniseries *Lonesome Dove,* based on the book by Larry McMurtry.

It's easy to see why many people relate to the story of *Lonesome Dove* as their own. In it they see their grandparents, or more abstractly the story of our country at the point its uniquely American character was laboring to be born. That the story is told so well is testament to the clear-eyed vision of Larry McMurtry as he penned his Pulitzer Prize–winning novel, and to the cast and crew who transcended the limits of television to bring his epic tale to the small screen with integrity intact. We recognize it not only as the most successful miniseries of all time; we celebrate it as the first time anyone got the story right.

The seventh floor of the Albert B. Alkek Library on the Texas State University–San Marcos campus may seem like an unlikely destination for a pilgrimage, yet the devoted journey here from around the globe. They come to the *Lonesome Dove* room to view relics from a time and place that, if not quite sacred, is revered as an authentic expression of friendship, honor, and the hardships of the Old West as it really was.

Upon entering the room, visitors may feel like Call ticking through the journey in his mind at the end of the film. It's a hell of a vision. The HAT CREEK CATTLE COMPANY sign is prominently displayed, and is flanked by mannequins wearing the costumes of Augustus "Gus" McCrae and Woodrow F. Call, two former Texas Rangers who set out on one last adventure to establish the first cattle operation in Montana. Jake Spoon's bandanna still contains traces of trail dust, and you can almost smell the despair in Lorena Wood's much-distressed dress. Gus's Colt Dragoon revolver is nearby, along with the arrows that killed him. The prop that was used for his body is a somber reminder of what was lost along the way, as is the cross from his grave and Deets's headstone.

"It's unusual to have so much documentation and memorabilia from a production," says Steve Davis, assistant curator of the collection. "It's a great example of how some of the magic of filmmaking is achieved."

Davis says he's seen visitors tear up at the site of Gus's body, a few who have come dressed as Gus and Call, and one who even named his children after the two characters. More than a few people make the *Lonesome Dove* room their first stop on a journey to retrace the cattle drive route from Texas to Montana. Some do it on horseback.

"It's heartwarming to work here and see the enormous number of people who come here—who make a pilgrimage, really—to be a part of the *Lonesome Dove* experience," Davis says. "The reaction is the same from people from all over the world. There's a common thread that unites—certainly people from Texas and the West feel that finally a Western told what it was really like. The film has struck a real chord in the American psyche."

Lonesome Dove began as a movie idea dreamed up by Larry McMurtry. In 1972, McMurtry wrote a screenplay treatment titled *Streets of Laredo* to star John Wayne, Henry Fonda, and James Stewart. Peter Bogdanovich was to direct. When the project failed to gain traction, McMurtry expanded the story into a long, multi-layered novel. Published in 1985, the book grabbed the imagination of critics and the public alike, spending twenty weeks atop the *New York Times* best-seller list and winning the Pulitzer Prize for fiction.

"*Streets of Laredo* didn't move forward because John Wayne wouldn't do it," McMurtry says. "He would have been the Call character in that story, and he didn't want to play what he considered to be an unlikable, hard-ass character. When he wouldn't do it, everyone else lost interest. I do have a family background that involved the cattle trade and trail drive tradition, which is probably the main reason I decided to write *Lonesome Dove*."

Shortly before the novel's publication, McMurtry sent a draft to Suzanne de Passe at Motown Productions. Motown optioned the film rights for $50,000 and CBS contracted to air *Lonesome Dove* as an eight-hour miniseries in four installments. All that remained was to find a way to adapt McMurtry's sweeping novel for television. That's when de Passe called on Bill Wittliff to write the screenplay. A Texas native like McMurtry, Wittliff felt a personal connection to the characters and events detailed in the novel.

"Like everybody, I thought it was an astonishing piece of work," Wittliff says. "From a personal response it was so much about my country, my people, but of course everybody felt that. That's one of the great things about [the novel] *Lonesome Dove*—everybody identified with it, and I absolutely did."

Wittliff, who was also co-executive producer with de Passe on the miniseries, wrote most of the screenplay during stints at his vacation home on South Padre Island. He would listen to the book on tape on the six-and-a-half-hour drive from his home in Austin.

"What was wonderful about that is that I was driving, not writing, and as I was listening I was making the pictures in my head. I got to see the whole film, or my version of it, making those trips down to South Padre. I would stay a week or so and write, and then I'd drive back and that would be another six and a half hours."

From the beginning, Wittliff knew that in order for the miniseries to be a success, he had to remain true to the book, and include all of its interconnected threads and characters.

"It's an epic story, and I never would have left out those subplots," Wittliff says. "They just gave it the richness and the size. There were some things that we filmed that did not make it to the final edit because we just didn't have time, but we squeezed in as much as we could."

Even though the time schedule was almost as tight as the budget, it was soon apparent that the *Lonesome Dove* project was buoyed by an enthusiasm unlike anything in television. The buzz reached every corner of the industry.

"It's Larry's story that got 'em," Wittliff says. "All the old clichés are true—like attracts in kind. It was a great book, it was a good script, and it attracted great artists. They were so taken by Larry's novel. I mean, we had people from all over the United States who drove in on their own nickel just to see if they could be extras. It wasn't so much they wanted to get something out of it; they wanted to put something in."

Diane Lane, who played Lorena Wood, remembers picking up on that feeling as soon as she arrived in Austin to begin filming.

"Even the people I met at the airport and the people who did the driving were all so meticulously into each character," she says. "I'd never seen anything like it."

That groundswell of intense appreciation for McMurtry's novel, published just a few years earlier, permeated every aspect of the miniseries.

"There was a reverence for the original material that was carried out by Bill in his writing of the screenplay," Lane says. "There was also great care taken in the casting, and when [Robert Duvall] signed on everybody couldn't wait to work with him, so we had top drawer people from the very get-go wanting to play every part."

Tommy Lee Jones, who played Call, says that the feeling among cast members was that the whole of *Lonesome Dove* was greater than the sum of its parts.

"Everybody that worked on the film cared a great deal about the authenticity of it. They felt it was mainly their responsibility to do right by the book," Jones says. "There was a social conscience at work that was unusual at that time in the world of television."

Says Wittliff: "Everybody was absolutely dedicated to it. Nobody ever said 'Oh, don't worry about it, it's just television.' We knew it was television, but everybody's attitude was 'Well, we're making a huge, epic movie, which as it happens is going to be shown on television.'"

Epic is right. Shot over sixteen weeks at three different locations, the project called for eighty-nine speaking parts, as many as six hundred head of cattle, ninety horses, and four sets of pigs. The conditions varied from one-hundred-degree heat on set in Del Rio, Texas, where the fictional town of Lonesome Dove was constructed, to freezing rain and snow in Angel Fire, New Mexico.

The remote shooting locations, budget, and time crunch, as well as the sheer scope of the project, required an effort far beyond the pale of an average television shoot.

Lane recalls slogging through creeks with a wary eye out for cottonmouths, as well as finding a scorpion in her petticoat while filming the scene where Gus entices her into the river.

"It got larger than life, definitely larger than the scale of normal filmmaking," Lane says. "But to be in the environs that the story takes place in was very affecting."

"I came in during the last three weeks and everyone was exhausted, having been in Texas and up in Angel Fire," says Anjelica Huston, who played Clara Allen. "On several occasions I had to rally the troops because I could see the pages disappearing from the script—we simply did not have the time to do everything."

But the motivation to bring the novel to life with the utmost authenticity, as well as the camaraderie of the cast and crew, overshadowed the numerous challenges.

We always said *Lonesome Dove* is the star, and I think everybody felt that," Wittliff says. "Every once in a while the movie god just points through the clouds and says, 'Regardless of what you do, this one's going to work.' There were so many places where this one could have fallen off the table. We were inventive in several places, but I don't think any place cheated the film."

Extraordinary luck also favored the production, such as when a freak snowstorm hit the community of Angel Fire in the middle of summer—on the same day the script called for a blizzard.

"We had snow machines and everything else ready to go and we woke up and the whole world was white," Wittliff says. "Let me tell you, stuff like that happened all the time. The whole thing was like walking through a miracle."

The first installment of *Lonesome Dove* aired on Sunday, February 5, 1989. That day blasts of arctic air blew down from Canada and seized most of the country in its icy grip. Many people hunkered down in their homes to wait out the cold, and more than a few tuned in to CBS at 9 p.m. to watch Gus McCrae and Woodrow Call begin their adventure. Those who weren't watching received a call from a friend or family member during the commercial breaks telling them to turn it on.

"Everybody stayed home and they started watching *Lonesome Dove,* and of course once you started then you couldn't quit," Wittliff says. "It was just unbelievable. People forget, at the time we did it the only thing deader than Westerns were miniseries, and this was a Western miniseries."

Lonesome Dove generated huge ratings for CBS, and the network aired the miniseries for a second time shortly thereafter. *Lonesome Dove* won seven Emmys and two Golden Globes that year, but the public response was even more telling.

"It was overwhelming—the reviews were all great and the mail from people all across the country poured into the office," Jones says. "We got heartfelt letters by the sack full from people who recognized their granddads and their fathers and their uncles in the story. They'd usually seen movies that were labeled 'Western,' and this seemed to defy that stereotype and be about real people and real places. They were very grateful to see the reality of their own history as opposed to some commercial distortion."

"The dialogue, the characters, the individualism of the people, the self-sufficiency, the ruggedness, it was all captured so well in *Lonesome Dove,*" says Ricky Schroder, who played Newt Dobbs. "It depicts a piece of our history as Americans that speaks to us. I think we all like to think about a time when life was simpler, when there was more black and white instead of gray."

In many ways, *Lonesome Dove* also set a new benchmark for the way Westerns looked and felt.

Says costume designer Van Broughton Ramsey: "I think that's one of the reasons why we're all still so proud of it twenty years later. *Lonesome Dove* was one of the first films to really show that the Old West is not about shoot 'em up, it's about facing the everyday problems in life, being thankful for what you have, and moving on the best way you know how."

It's that simple, universal message, as well as the realistic portrayal of humanity in all its extremes, that keeps *Lonesome Dove* a fan favorite more than twenty years after its original release. And why, despite a lack of modern special effects and fast-paced sizzle, the film continues to resonate with a new generation of viewers.

"I wish Robert Urich [who played Jake Spoon] was still with us so he could experience the gratitude from all of the fans for his work," says Lane. "But the wonderful gift of film is that the grave has no sway. You are forever in that encapsulated bubble and that's a brilliant gift that film gives back to people who work in that medium. Your work can live forever."

Don't Fence Me In

1945; directed by John English; written by Dorrell McGowan and Stuart E. McGowan; starring Roy Rogers, Trigger, Gabby Hayes, and Dale Evans

By 1945, Roy Rogers had been singing and appearing in Saturday matinees for ten years. And for the past three, the gorgeous songstress, his wife Dale Evans, had been appearing at his side. From the title song by Cole Porter with its fantastic lyrics—"Gaze at the moon till I lose my senses"—to the other equally famous songs by the Sons of the Pioneers, "The Last Roundup" and "Tumbling Tumbleweeds" ("See them tumbling down . . ."), *Don't Fence Me In* is a classic from start to finish. The great cowboy and cowgirl duo and their famous horses (Trigger and Buttermilk) were joined by the great

Gabby Hayes, a Shakespearean actor with a knack for playing the curmudgeon in this funny musical film, a true star among the B Westerns by singing cowboys.

The plot is quite humorous. Dale Evans plays an eastern magazine reporter hot on the trail of the true story of the mysterious Wildcat Kelly, who has supposedly been dead and buried for years. She suspects that Gabby Hayes knows more than he is telling when she meets up with him and with Roy Rogers . . . and mayhem ensues, but it all works out well in the end.

Roy Rogers on Trigger COURTESY OF THE ROY ROGERS–DALE EVANS FAMILY AND MUSEUM

Olivia de Havilland publicity still for *Dodge City,* 1939 MPTVIMAGES.COM

Dodge City

1939; directed by Michael Curtiz; written by Robert Buckner; starring Errol Flynn, Olivia De Havilland, and Ann Sheridan

When it was released in 1939, this gorgeous Technicolor Flynn and De Havilland collaboration, directed by the great Michael Curtiz (*Casablanca*) was overshadowed by a few other movies that make it onto "Greatest" lists, including ours. It was the year of *Gone With the Wind*, *The Wizard of Oz*, and *Stagecoach*. But this great movie about the wickedest town in the West holds up to the others and stands the test of time.

This was Flynn's first Western, and he was originally concerned that American audiences wouldn't believe him as a dashing hero of the frontier, but he'd go on to make several Westerns, often paired with the gorgeous De Havilland, whose feisty Abbie Irving in *Dodge City* is the antithesis of the meek and genteel Melanie Wilkes, whom she also played that year.

The town of Dodge City desperately needs an upright citizen like Wade Hatton (Errol Flynn) to come in and take over as marshal and restore justice and order. But he's unwilling to take on the job, which is further complicated by the fact that he fancies Abbie, a newspaper reporter who blames Wade for the death of her younger brother. A great saloon brawl and a satisfying "into the sunset" ending may seem like clichés, but this is a great movie that originated those "clichés," and followers can only try to live up to it.

The Big Sky

1952; directed by Howard Hawks; written by Dudley Nichols, Ray Buffum, and DeVallon Scott, and based on the novel by A. B. Guthrie Jr.; starring Kirk Douglas, Dewey Martin, and Elizabeth Threatt

The Big Sky, set in the heady early days of trade along the Missouri River, is a classic buddy film and an epic tale of adventure on the trail of fortune. It's 1832, and mountain man Jim Deakins (Kirk Douglas) has met up with Boone Caudill (Dewey Martin) in the remote wilderness. They become friends and travel together to the Missouri River in search of Boone's Uncle Zeb. After a brawl with fur traders lands them in jail—fortuitously right next to Zeb, who arranges for their bail—they join an expedition to travel the two thousand miles up the river to trade with the Blackfeet.

Along for the journey is Teal Eye (Elizabeth Threatt) a young Blackfoot woman, the daughter of a chief, whom Zeb wants to exploit in the trade negotiations. A rival fur-trading company keeps trying to thwart the heroes' efforts along the river, the Crow Indians attack, and a shootout with bad guys eventually leaves them free to reach their goal. Oh, and Boone and Teal Eye fall in love and he chooses to stay with her and her people.

While it isn't a terribly faithful interpretation of the great Guthrie novel of the West, the movie stands on its own merits and is one of the greatest "frontier" Westerns ever made. Arthur Hunnicutt received an Oscar nomination for his performance as Uncle Zeb, and the scenery is beautiful because it was actually filmed on location along the Snake River—a rarity in those studio days. One of those movies that very few people seem to know about, it definitely earns a spot in the top fifty on this list.

Ride the High Country

1962; directed by Sam Peckinpah; written by N. B. Stone Jr.; starring Randolph Scott, Joel McCrea, and Mariette Hartley

Starring Joel McCrea, Randolph Scott, Ron Starr, Edgar Buchanan, and Mariette Hartley, *Ride the High Country* is generally recognized to be director Sam Peckinpah's first great film. But it is also Randolph Scott's last film role—the iconic hero of the silver screen had decided to retire after it was made.

In the movie two old friends, ex-lawmen Gil Westrum (Randolph Scott) and Steve Judd (Joel McCrea) have reunited to take the job of guarding a shipment of gold that is being transported to civilization from a mining camp. Along with a young sidekick named Heck Longtree (Ron Starr), Westrum is actually planning to steal the gold and spends the trip out of the mountains trying to convince Judd to come in on the deal.

Both men, now aging and unable to get work as lawmen, have reached the point of needing either the hard, nearly thankless job of escorting treasure as paid guards or turning to the life of crime that they once valiantly struggled against.

The themes of honor, ideals, and the difficulty of maintaining both in the face of circumstance are classic Peckinpah signatures. In the case of *Ride the High Country,* which wasn't immediately a hit in the United States but has grown in stature in the intervening decades, the plight of the two aging lawmen stands in for the last days of the Old West and the dismantling of its heroes.

Open Range

2003; directed by Kevin Costner; written by Craig Storper, based on the novel by Lauran Paine; starring Kevin Costner, Robert Duvall, and Annette Bening

Set in Montana in 1882, *Open Range* interprets the "range wars" of the late nineteenth century that pitted the cattlemen who wanted free access to water and grass on the open plains against the newly developing species of land barons who were fencing off country and setting up their own little empires.

Cattleman "Boss" Spearman (Robert Duvall) and his hired hands Charley Waite (Kevin Costner), Mose (Abraham Benrubi), and Button (Diego Luna) are driving a herd when they run afoul of a ruthless land baron who has designs on the cattle herd that the men are driving. After a fierce battle between the free rangers and the land baron in which one of the men is killed, another is injured, and their dog is also killed, Charley and Boss vow revenge.

Though the movie got good reviews when it opened in theaters, it was only a modest financial success—but it won the 2004 Western Heritage Award and was nominated for a Golden Satellite Award, an MTV Movie Award (Diego Luna), and a Motion Picture Sound Editors Award. And we see it as a top-fifty film that will absolutely stand the test of time due to its classic storyline and its interpretation of the events that changed and closed the West.

The Westerner

1940; directed by William Wyler; written by Jo Swerling, Niven Busch, Stuart N. Lake, W. R. Burnett, Lillian Hellman, and Oliver La Farge; starring Gary Cooper and Walter Brennan

The infamous Judge Roy Bean, the hanging judge of Texas, is the villain of this William Wyler Western starring Walter Brennan as Judge Bean himself. Between Brennan and Gary Cooper, who plays a young feller who "just doesn't look like a horse thief," and the great Wyler's direction, this is one of those terrific pre-war Westerns that doesn't try to be more than it is but has such a wonderful story, great characters, and skilled direction that it remains a favorite to this day.

After Cole's hanging is delayed because he's able to convince the judge that he knows Lillie Langtry, the object of the judge's obsession, he manages to get in the middle of the range war fomenting between Roy Bean and homesteaders moving into the region—and then gets himself appointed sheriff, and sets out to take down the judge once and for all, eventually doing so at a Langtry performance.

Brennan's performance as Bean earned him his third Academy Award for Best Supporting Actor. James Basevi and Stuart N. Lake also received nominations for the Academy Award for Best Art Direction (Black-and-White) and Best Story, respectively.

Last of the Mohicans

1992; directed by Michael Mann; adapted for the screen by John L. Balderson, based on the novel by James Fenimore Cooper; starring Daniel Day Lewis, Madeleine Stowe, and Wes Studi

In early eighteenth-century colonial America, upstate New York was the Wild West—and this movie version of the classic James Fenimore Cooper novel is a great Western film. British and French troops battle against each other aided by various Indian war parties, and the independent loner develops a romantic relationship with the daughter of a British officer while fighting for the people who adopted him, the great Mohicans.

Gorgeous filmmaking and cinematography, and a score that sets the heart racing, make this a great film that really resonates across the genre spectrum. One of the best films ever made as well as a great Western.

❋ THE TEN GREATEST ❋
GUNFIGHTER
⤏ MOVIES OF ALL TIME ⤎

Most of these make our larger list, too—but we think that the gunfights and the gunfighters that distinguish them are worth yet another look:

10. *The Virginian* (1929)—The 1929 version is the best film adaptation of Owen Wister's classic novel.

9. *Western Union* (1941)—Randolph Scott shines as one of two outlaw brothers who lock horns.

8. *My Darling Clementine* (1946)—The first feature film to depict the Gunfight at the OK Corral.

7. *The Wild Bunch* (1969)—The climactic gunfight in Sam Peckinpah's classic gets the award for most-ever amount of slung lead.

6. *Shane* (1953)—The showdown between Shane (Alan Ladd) and adversary Wilson (Jack Palance) is for the ages.

5. *Appaloosa* (2008)—Perhaps the most realistic of all the top ten gunfighter films.

4. *Tombstone* (1993)—This popular modern retelling of an oft-told tale has unforgettable action scenes.

3. *The Shootist* (1976)—Finishing high, and climbing in reputation, this was John Wayne's last picture.

2. *High Noon* (1952)—Also ranked high on the list, High Noon builds suspense until the clock strikes twelve.

1. *Open Range* (2003)—Costner's best Western keeps winning converts.

The Shootist

1976; directed by Don Siegel; written by Miles Hood Swarthout and Scott Hale, based on the novel by Glendon Swarthout; Starring John Wayne, Lauren Bacall, James Stewart, and Ron Howard

It's appropriate that John Wayne's last Western—his last movie—tells the story of a gunfighter in the waning days of the Old West (1901) who finds out he's dying of cancer. In real life Wayne had beaten cancer once and he delivers each line with a heart-wrenching conviction that makes this movie a tearjerker from start to finish. When he says to Ron Howard's character, "I won't be wronged, I won't be insulted, and I won't be laid a hand on. I do not do these things to others and require the same of them," it's hard to say whether that's the character or the Duke speaking. What a fine way to end a remarkable career.

The movie starts with a montage of Wayne's earlier Westerns, working together to depict the life of the legendary gunman he portrays in the movie. It ends up being one of the greatest tributes to the great man. After finishing *The Shootist,* Wayne would live only another three years—in the end his cancer returned and caught up with him.

John Wayne, Lauren Bacall, and Ron Howard, *The Shootist,* Paramount, 1976, © 1978 David Sutton MPTVIMAGES.COM

Destry Rides Again

1939; directed by George Marshall; written by Felix Jackson, Gertrude Purcell, and Henry Myers, loosely based on the novel by Max Brand; starring James Stewart and Marlene Dietrich

If all you know of Marlene Dietrich is the spot-on and hilarious spoof character Lili Von Schtupp from *Blazing Saddles,* then you should immediately rent this top-fifty entry to see the real deal. Marlene Dietrich and Jimmy Stewart, paired together in the great *Destry Rides Again,* a Western comedy satire in its own right, takes the classic Western and tweaks its nose. But it also stands up as a Western with its saloon, its sheriff, and its beautiful dance-hall girl Frenchie all thrown together in a comedic plot that's almost Shakespearean in its twist and turns—and there's music as well!

Overshadowed by the other 1939 classics, *Gone With the Wind, Dodge City, Stagecoach,* and *The Wizard of Oz, Destry Rides Again* didn't get a single Academy Award nomination.

———————

It's appropriate that this American Western was Marlene Dietrich's first movie after she became an American citizen.

———————

Marlene Dietrich and James Stewart, *Destry Rides Again,* Universal Pictures, 1939 MPTV
IMAGES.COM

The Professionals

1966; directed by Richard Brooks; written by Richard Brooks, based on the novel by Frank O'Rourke; starring Burt Lancaster, Lee Marvin, and Robert Ryan

Nominated for three Academy Awards, including Best Director, Best Writing (Adapted Screenplay), and Best Cinematography, *The Professionals* is a classic Western that reaches beyond its genre, interpreting the Frank O'Rourke novel about a rancher who hires four men to rescue his kidnapped wife.

The wife of rancher J. W. Grant (Ralph Bellamy), Maria (Claudia Cardinale), has been snatched by Jesus Raza (Jack Palance), a bandit who was once a Mexican Revolutionary leader. The four men who are on his trail to rescue Maria each have their own specialty, sort of an Old West A-Team. Henry "Rico" Fardan (Lee Marvin) is a weapons specialist, Bill Dolworth (Burt Lancaster) is an explosives expert, Hans Ehrengard (Robert Ryan) is a skilled horse wrangler, and Jake Sharp (Woody Strode) is a scout with traditional Apache skills. The four men rescue Maria and then uncover a surprising truth that leads to more mayhem.

———•◦•———

Claudia Cardinale's stunt double was badly injured during a scene where Maria escapes through a canyon that has been booby-trapped with dynamite. Afterward, Cardinale, who had never ridden a horse before, performed the stunt herself.

———•◦•———

Tall in the Saddle

1944; directed by Edwin L. Marin; written by Michael Hogan, Paul Fix, and Gordon Ray Young; starring John Wayne, Ella Raines, and Ward Bond

An old-fashioned Western with great scenery, beautiful women, and some of the best Western actors of all time, *Tall in the Saddle* opens the second half of this list with a bang—or with a crack of the whip wielded by the lovely Ella Raines as Arly Harolday, the spitfire woman rancher who is John Wayne's love/hate interest in the movie.

Rocklin (John Wayne) is a stranger who has arrived in a Western town to go to work for the KC Ranch. The problem is that the rancher who hired him has been murdered and the ranch has been inherited by a lovely Easterner, Clara Cardell (Audry Long). The stranger seems to have a lot of secrets—and a big problem working for women—but the rest of the town has secrets, too, especially the obviously oily and probably crooked judge played by Ward Bond.

Ride Lonesome

1959; directed by Budd Boetticher; written by Burt Kennedy; starring Randolph Scott and James Coburn

Bounty hunter Ben Brigade (Randolph Scott) has captured wanted murderer Billy John (James Best) and is taking his prey to Santa Cruz where he's to receive justice at the end of a rope. Along the way he stops a band of Indians from murdering the wife of a stage-stop owner and meets up with two sidekicks/outlaws named Whit and Sam Boone who want to help deliver Billy John so that they can share in the reward money.

Billy John's brother Frank (Lee Van Cleef) is hot on the trail of the bounty hunters and has no intention of letting them make their way to Santa Cruz.

The Plainsman

1936; directed by Cecil B. DeMille; written by Courtney Ryley Cooper, Frank J. Wilstach, Jeanie MacPherson, Waldemar Young, Harold Lamb, Lynn Riggs, and Grover Jones; starring Gary Cooper, Jean Arthur, and James Ellison

Populated with some of the most legendary characters from the myth of the Old West, *The Plainsman* is a look at that myth as only the master showman Cecil B. DeMille could produce it. Calamity Jane, Buffalo Bill Cody, Wild Bill Hickok, and General George Armstrong Custer all find their way into the story of a plot by gun manufacturers to sell weapons to Native Americans after the Civil War—and only Wild Bill Hickok (Gary Cooper) can save Calamity Jane (Jean Arthur) from her kidnappers and help stop the gun trafficking.

The movie is imaginative about American history to say the least, but the scene that recreates the Battle of Little Bighorn, shot on location in Montana and featuring thousands of Native Americans as extras, is worth the cost of the DVD.

Cat Ballou

1965; directed by Elliot Silverstein; written by Walter Newman and Frank Pierson, based on the novel *The Ballad of Cat Ballou* by Roy Chanslor; starring Jane Fonda and Lee Marvin

All Cat (Catherine) Ballou wants is to become a schoolteacher, but when her father is threatened by a gunman working for the railroad magnate who wants her family's farm, she hires a gunman of her own, the legendary Kid Shelleen, who turns out to be the drunkest gunfighter in the West, to come protect him.

Jane Fonda sparkles as the feisty Cat Ballou, but Lee Marvin, playing the dual roles of Kid Shelleen and the fast-drawing villain Tim Strawn (aka Silvernose), absolutely earned his Best Actor Academy Award with his combination of menace and impeccable comic timing, and stunt riding (he's actually sideways in several scenes). When he accepted that award he famously said, "Half of this Oscar belongs to a horse someplace out in the valley."

Throughout the movie, minstrels played by Nat King Cole and Stubby Kaye sing "The Ballad of Cat Ballou" in between scenes, narrating the story as it unfolds. A comedy that highlights the best of Western movie making without spoofing it or itself, *Cat Ballou* is one of the Farrelly brothers' favorite movies—they've said that the Balladeers in their film *There's Something About Mary* were inspired by the minstrels in Cat Ballou.

———•-•———

Nat King Cole died of lung cancer several months before *Cat Ballou* was released in theaters.

———•-•———

Jane Fonda, *Cat Ballou*, Columbia, 1965 MPTVIMAGES.COM

SCREEN HORSES

❧ AND THEIR HEROES ☙

BY BRAD PROWSE FOR *AMERICAN COWBOY*

In the movie-making business, the introduction of sound in 1929 gave birth, five years later, to the singing cowboy. And the idea of the singing cowboy seemed to strike the public's fancy. From then until the late 1940s, most B Westerns featured a hero who could sing—Roy Rogers, Gene Autry—or a sidekick who could.

But even more indispensable than a sidekick, singing or otherwise, was a faithful horse—one that usually had an IQ somewhat higher than that of the sidekick. Not only would this horse be able to run faster and jump higher than any other horse in the movie, it could also loosen rope bonds with its teeth, go for help, deliver messages, and—at critical moments toward the end of the picture—put its head between the hero and the heroine, thereby sparing the kids at the Saturday matinee any "mushy" stuff.

The first star to make it big in the singing cowboy trade, Gene Autry, made ninety-one movies between 1934 and 1953 and went on to host a TV series. All featured a horse, Champion, a big sorrel with a blaze face and three white stockings.

According to *Back in the Saddle Again,* Autry's autobiography, the first Champion—born in 1927 and named Lindy—was previously used by Tom Mix in his road shows. This horse died in 1943 or 1944 while Autry was serving in the army. The second Champion was a Tennessee Walker that probably was bought from the Hudkins Stables, supplier of horses to the movies.

Autry had hired John Agee, Lindy's trainer, to look after his stables. To prepare Champion for road work, Agee set up speakers and subjected him to recordings of loud band music, crowd noises, and applause until he would remain calm under the most trying of circumstances.

At a Pennsylvania engagement, Champion fell from a collapsing stage and ended up on his side with one hoof hung up in the debris above. Cradling the big horse's head in his lap, Autry comforted Champion. The horse allowed the stage crew to extricate him. It was found he had suffered only a scratch and after a five-minute break Champion went on with the show—a champion, indeed.

The second Champion was used extensively in rodeo and personal appearance work. A final Champion, probably the third horse so named

but perhaps the fourth, was used for TV work. This last Champion died in 1990 on Autry's Melody Ranch in Southern California.

Roy Rogers was the only other movie cowboy to attain the level of popularity of Gene Autry. And, like Autry, he had a horse that was almost as popular as he was—Trigger.

Most accounts—but not all—put the birth of Trigger in 1932, foaled in Santa Cietro,

COURTESY OF THE ROY ROGERS–DALE EVANS FAMILY AND MUSEUM

California, on a ranch part-owned by Bing Crosby and managed by Roy Cloud, a noted horse breeder. Trigger—then a palomino stallion named Golden Cloud—was sold by Cloud to the Hudkins Stables, where Rogers purchased him. There are several amounts mentioned in his purchase. In one account $300, in another, $2,500.

Trigger is supposed to have been taught at least sixty tricks. He died in 1965, aged around thirty-three.

The movie cowboy and his horse appeared with *The Great Train Robbery* in 1903. Perhaps the earliest Western star to have his "own" horse was William S. Hart, who listed his horse, Fritz, in the credits. As Hart's dark and brooding films fell into disfavor, Tom Mix introduced the flamboyant cowboy, dressed as if for a circus act. Mix made his horse, Tony, a star and the animal was trained to perform a number of tricks.

By the time the singing cowboy came along in the mid-1930s, a "favorite" horse and a sidekick were part of the retinue the cowboy hero took with him on his adventures.

In film after film, these celluloid examples of truth and justice galloped their mounts after bad guys, Gene Autry on Champion, Roy Rogers on Trigger, William "Hopalong Cassidy" Boyd on Topper, and so on. Some of the horses were owned by the cowboy star—as were Champion and Trigger. Others were regularly assigned from the pool of studio mounts. There were over fifty western movie stars that used a "pet" horse, identified with the star, as opposed to riding an ordinary unnamed mount as most of the rest of the cast did.

The movie Western is seldom seen these days, and the singing cowboy and his horse are relegated to the video stores. Today the kids have their Luke Skywalkers and Ninja Turtles—but they never had Gene or Roy or those magnificent steeds they rode across the silver screen. Their loss.

The Tall T

1957; directed by Budd Boetticher; written by Elmore Leonard and Burt Kennedy, based on the short story "The Captives" by Elmore Leonard; starring Randolph Scott and Richard Boone

Nobody writes dialogue like Elmore Leonard, and the word play in Budd Boetticher's interpretation of his short story "The Captives" is a highlight of this light-hearted adventure movie that takes a dramatic twist.

After losing his horse in a bet, Pat Brennan (Randolph Scott) hitches a ride on a stagecoach carrying newlyweds Willard and Doretta Mims. The coach and its passengers fall into the hands of a trio of outlaws headed by a man named Usher who decides to hold Doretta for ransom—her father is a copper baron. In the end, Randolph Scott saves the day and gets the girl in a movie that exposes greed and cowardice and takes pains to point out that the guys in black hats aren't the only bad guys out there.

Jesse James

1939; directed by Henry King; written by Nunnally Johnson, Hal Long, Gene Fowler, and Curtis Kenyon; starring Tyrone Power, Henry Fonda, and Randolph Scott

Not the first, and certainly not the last, movie to tell the story of the notorious bandit brothers Frank and Jesse James, this Henry King version of the tale nonetheless gets high marks for its stylish direction, glamour, and star-quality performances by heartthrob Tyrone Power, brilliant character actor Henry Fonda, and the legendary Randolph Scott.

The James brothers are clearly underdogs forced to turn to outlawry when circumstances require it. In this version of the story, they're seeking revenge after railroad agents forcibly evict the James family from their farm.

———•—•———

The Return of Frank James (1940) features Henry Fonda reprising his role as Jesse's brother Frank and the film debut of Gene Tierney as a reporter.

———•—•———

JESSE JAMES ON THE SILVER SCREEN

He is one of the most often interpreted real-life characters ever to appear on the silver screen. Of all the actors to portray Jesse James over the last century, from Audie Murphy to Brad Pitt, one wonders which he would have approved the most. This list doesn't even include the made-for-TV movies.

1908	*The James Boys in Missouri* Harry McCabe	
1921	*Jesse James under the Black Flag* Jesse James Jr.	
1921	*Jesse James as the Outlaw* Jesse James Jr.	
1927	*Jesse James* Fred Thomspson	
1939	*Days of Jesse James* Don "Red" Barry	
1939	*Jesse James* Tyrone Power	
1940	*The Return of Frank James* Tyrone Power	
1941	*Bad Men of Missouri* Alan Baxter	
1941	*Jesse James at Bay* Roy Rogers	
1942	*The Remarkable Andrew* Rod Cameron	
1943	*The Kansan* George Reeves	

1946	*Badman's Territory* Lawrence Tierney
1947	*Jesse James Rides Again* Clayton Moore
1948	*Adventures of Frank and Jesse James* Clayton Moore
1949	*I Shot Jesse James* Reed Hadley
1949	*The James Brothers of Missouri* Keith Richards
1949	*Fighting Men of the Plains* Dale Robertson
1950	*Kansas Raiders* Audie Murphy
1951	*The Great Missouri Raid* MacDonald Carey
1951	*Best of the Badmen* Lawrence Tierney
1953	*The Woman They Almost Lynched* Ben Cooper
1953	*The Great Jesse James Raid* Willard Parker (adult Jesse), Tommy Walker (young Jesse)

1954 *Jesse James' Women*
Don "Red" Barry

1955 *Outlaw Treasure*
Harry Lauter

1957 *Hell's Crossroads*
Henry Brandon

1957 *The True Story of Jesse James*
Robert Wagner

1959 *Alias Jesse James*
Wendell Corey

1960 *Young Jesse James*
Ray Stricklyn

1965 *The Outlaws Is Coming*
Wayne Mack

1966 *Jesse James Meets Frankenstein's Daughter* John Lupton

1969 *A Time for Dying*
Audie Murphy

1972 *The Great Northfield Minnesota Raid*
Robert Duvall

1977 *Another Man, Another Chance*
Christopher Lloyd

1980 *The Long Riders*
James Keach

1990 *Stairway to Paradise*
Jeff James

W.I. Swain's Western spectacular production, Jesse James—Theatrical Production 1880s LIBRARY OF CONGRESS

1994 *Frank & Jesse*
Rob Lowe

1995 *Cyber Vengeance*
Craig Teper

2001 *American Outlaws*
Colin Farrell

2003 *Outlaws of Missouri*
Bruce McDonald

2007 *The Assassination of Jesse James by the Coward Robert Ford*
Brad Pitt

Little Big Man

1970; directed by Arthur Penn; written by Calder Willingham, based on the novel by Thomas Berger; starring Dustin Hoffman, Faye Dunaway, and Chief Dan George

In this picaresque comedy/drama about a Caucasian boy raised by the Cheyenne nation during the nineteenth century, Dustin Hoffman plays 121-year-old Jack Crabb recalling his life with the Cheyenne tribe and his experiences with Wild Bill Hickok and General George Armstrong Custer for the benefit of a curious historian.

At turns very funny and horribly tragic, in its depiction of the Indian wars of the nineteenth century *Little Big Man* subtly, or not so subtly, protests America's involvement in the Vietnam War. It's truly a revisionist Western, portraying the Native Americans in a sympathetic fashion—especially as compared to earlier portrayals in Western films. And it takes considerable liberty with American history, putting events out of order and misrepresenting participants' roles in battles for the sake of humor. But it makes its point—and it's great entertainment.

———•—•———

Dustin Hoffman holds the record for portraying the greatest age span of a single character, playing Jack Crabb from the age of 17 to 121—104 years.

———•—•———

Riders of the Purple Sage

1925; directed by Lynn Reynolds; written by Edfrid A. Bingham, based on the novel by Zane Grey; starring Tom Mix, Beatrice Burnham, and Arthur Morrison

Riders of the Purple Sage was one of Zane Grey's greatest novels, and with Tom Mix at the helm of this early silent version it becomes a successful movie—though it takes considerably liberty with the complex and layered plot of the original book. Tom Mix was Hollywood's first great cowboy hero and the tone he set in his silent movies paved the way for generations to come—the same could be said of the novel, which framed the Western fiction genre by establishing many of the themes, characters, and mores that characterize the genre to this day.

Tom Mix plays Jim Carson, whose sister Millie (Beatrice Burnham) and her daughter Bessie are kidnapped by the henchmen of the nefarious lawyer Lew Walters, and he sets off to find them. Changing his name to Lassiter and gaining a reputation as gunfighter, he tracks them across the West, eventually joining up with rancher Jane Witherspoon in her fight against the rustling Riders of the Purple Sage.

The Alamo

1960; directed by John Wayne; written by James Edward Grant; starring John Wayne, Richard Widmark, and Laurence Harvey

For years the great Hollywood superstar and leading man, John Wayne, had wanted to make an epic Western about the tragic events that occurred at the Alamo in 1836. In order to fulfill his very specific vision of what the movie should entail, he elected to produce and direct the movie himself—agreeing to act in the movie as well in order to secure financing from United Artists.

The story of the Alamo has been told many times on film, just as the Battle of the Little Big Horn has been. And, as frequently happens in film versions of the later event, some liberties are taken with the story in order to turn it into good filmmaking. However, the set, built in Texas, was one of the most authentic movie sets ever created. Thousands and thousands of adobe bricks were made by hand to create the mission and other buildings, and the set was used many times in Westerns in later years.

Though the film performed well at the box office and received numerous Academy Award nominations, John Wayne lost his personal investment in the movie because it was so expensive to make. Eventually, he sold his rights to the film to United Artists.

The Far Country

1954; directed by Anthony Mann; written by Borden Chase; starring James Stewart, Ruth Roman, and Harry Morgan

Jimmy Stewart starred in five classic Western movies directed by Anthony Mann, and in all five he rode the same horse and wore the same hat. In this film, Jeff Webster (Jimmy Stewart) decides to drive a herd of cattle to Dawson City at the start of the Klondike gold rush—a surefire moneymaking proposition. On the way, he runs afoul of a local judge and spends the rest of the movie trying hard to stay out of trouble—and not succeeding very well. In the end, forced to take sides in the growing lawless community, he kills the villain—but it's the cinematography, great direction, and fantastic performances that hold you riveted through the story.

Three Godfathers

1935; directed by Richard Boleslawski; written by Edward E. Paramore, based on the novel by Peter B. Kyne; starring Chester Morris, Lewis Stone, and Walter Brennan

Billed as a great Western desert epic, *Three Godfathers* is a classic fish out of water (or in this case, three fish out of water) story set in a truly arid landscape with all of the trappings of a great Western adventure. Four outlaws ride into the tiny town of New Jerusalem to rob the bank, and only three escape, followed into the surrounding desert by the posse hot on their trail. When they finally make it to a water hole in the bleak landscape, they don't find water—but they do find a wagon and a dying mother and her baby.

The next morning, they find that their horses are dead and they decide they have no choice but to walk back to New Jerusalem. Two of the bandits want to take the baby back with them but one wants nothing to do with it. The men's interactions with the infant as they head back toward town and trouble offer comic relief from the desperation they all feel—and the mix of danger, poignancy, and the unlikely situation has inspired numerous copies over the years, including a John Ford version starring John Wayne.

Appaloosa

2008; directed by Ed Harris; written by Robert Knott and Ed Harris, based on the novel by Robert Parker; starring Ed Harris and Viggo Mortenson

Ed Harris stars in, co-wrote, and directed *Appaloosa,* a tribute to earlier Western films that gets nearly everything right. The strong story and intriguing characters—characters with more depth than the usual stereotypes—make this one of the great films of the first decade of the twenty-first century and a great Western for all time.

Based on a novel by Robert Parker, *Appaloosa* tells the story of Virgil Cole and Everett Hitch, two lawmen for hire in the little frontier town of Appaloosa. In a familiar story to those who appreciate Westerns, a local rancher has shot and killed the previous marshal for standing up to him and now rides roughshod over the town. And essentially, the movie is a tale about what justice means in a time when every man must decide for himself where he stands along the spectrum of right and wrong. But it's the friendship between Cole and Hitch that provides the movie's heart.

Forty Guns

1957; directed by Samuel Fuller; written by Samuel Fuller; starring Barbara Stanwyck, Barry Sullivan, and Dean Jagger

The great Barbara Stanwyck had a gift for comedy, a gift from melodrama, and—as TV audiences would see from 1965 to 1969 on *The Big Valley*—a gift for playing strong, authoritative Western women. In *Forty Guns,* Stanwyck plays Arizona rancher Jessica Drummond, a woman who runs the county with her posse of forty hired guns.

When the new U.S. Marshal, Griff Bonnell (Barry Sullivan) arrives in town, he is aiming to arrest one of the eponymous guns and also takes on Jessica Drummond's drunken lout of a brother. Inevitably, the marshal and the rancher meet, fight, and then become romantic.

As directed by Sam Fuller, the movie takes utmost advantage of the CinemaScope format with sweeping scenes of horses thundering across the horizon and even a prodigiously long dining room table presided over by Stanwyck. Some critics have called this movie more style than substance. In our opinion, it has plenty of both.

———•—•———

In one scene, Jessica Drummond is dragged along a street by a horse. And it's actually Barbara Stanwyck who's being dragged. Her stunt woman refused to do the trick, saying it was too dangerous, but the forty-nine-year-old Stanwyck had no such hesitation, escaping with some bruises and scrapes.

———•—•———

3:10 to Yuma

1957; directed by Delmer Daves; written by Halsted Welles, based on the story by Elmore Leonard; starring Glenn Ford, Van Heflin, and Felicia Farr

Before Russell Crow and Christian Bale there was Glenn Ford, the outlaw leader and psychopathic killer, and Van Heflin, the down-on-his-luck small town rancher, around whom the suspense in *3:10 to Yuma* circles.

The outlaw Ben Wade (Ford) has been captured in a small town and is scheduled to be on the 3:10 train to Yuma, where he will presumably be hanged for his crimes. Rancher Dan Evans (Heflin) agrees to serve as his guard, delivering him to Yuma for the reward money that will save his family's ranch.

Set in the parched desert landscape, what is essentially a tale of a battle of wills between the two men becomes one of the greatest Western movies ever—and one of the greatest stories of suspense. Will Dan Evans succumb to the mind games of the villain and take his bribe—or will he hold fast to the virtues of civilization?

Felicia Farr and Glenn Ford, *3:10 to Yuma*, Columbia Pictures, 1957

Gunfight at the O.K. Corral

1957; directed by John Sturges; written by Leon Uris and based on an article by George Scullin; starring Burt Lancaster and Kirk Douglas

Like the numerous other movies about the shootout at the O.K. Corral, this movie is based on a real event that took place near Tombstone, in what is now Arizona, on October 26, 1881, when Wyatt Earp and his fellow lawmen brothers joined forces with the notorious gunfighter Doc Holliday to end the reign of terror of Old Man Clanton and his Cowboys organization.

As pure entertainment, this depiction of the gun battle lives up to the myth of the real event, even as it departs from actual history. It doesn't get much better than this. After its 1957 release, the movie was nominated for two Academy Awards for sound and editing. But what elevates this movie to greatness is the cast. Burt Lancaster is brilliant as the tortured Wyatt Earp and Kirk Douglas's Doc Holliday is one of his greatest roles.

Sergeant Rutledge

1960; directed by John Ford; written by James Warner Bellah and Willis Goldbeck; starring Jeffrey Hunter, Constance Towers, and Billie Burke

Like many of the great John Ford Westerns of the 1950s and 1960s, *Sergeant Rutledge* was filmed on location in Monument Valley, Utah, but the real drama of this story takes place in the courtroom where Sergeant Braxton Rutledge (Woody Strode), a "Buffalo Soldier" serving with the 9th Cavalry, is court-martialed for raping and murdering the daughter of his commanding officer and then murdering the commanding officer as well. The circumstantial evidence is against him and he deserts after the killings.

The story in the movie unfolds through a series of flashbacks revealed as each of the witnesses steps up to tell what they know during the trial. A respected member of the cavalry before the trial, he stands before an all-white military court to protest his innocence and the prejudices that he faces are revealed.

Little Big Horn

1951; directed by Charles Marquis Warren; written by Charles Marquis Warren, based on the screenplay by Harold Shumate; starring Lloyd Bridges, John Ireland, and Marie Windsor

This is one of those great Westerns of the mid-twentieth century that's now become hard to find on video or DVD, characterized by terrific performances and taking a different approach to a well-known story from history.

Most of *Little Big Horn* focuses on the events leading up to Custer's last stand. A small band of cavalry has learned that the Sioux are planning to ambush Custer and they are on their way to warn him, but as they make their way toward the famous boy general and his troops, sharpshooters pick them off one by one.

The focus on character rather than spectacle in this telling of the events of that summer's Indian wars is largely successful because of the great, believable performances by Lloyd Bridges and John Ireland. You find yourself absorbed by the story and deeply concerned for the fate of all involved before the movie and the events of history play out on screen.

Seven Men From Now

1956; directed by Bud Boetticher; written by Burt Kennedy; starring Randolph Scott, Gail Russell, and Lee Marvin

Ex-sheriff Ben Stride (Randolph Scott) has become obsessed with tracking the seven men who held up a Wells Fargo office and killed his wife, tormented by his feelings of responsibility for her death. As he searches, he meets a married couple heading west for California and two ne'er-do-wells, Masters (Lee Marvin) and Clete, who know that Stride is after the bandits and plan to make off with the loot once he's found them.

As they travel, they have a close encounter with one of the Wells Fargo robbers who is being chased by Indians. Stride, not realizing his identity, actually rescues him and then is nearly killed by him before Masters shoots him in the back. As it turns out, though, almost no one in the small party heading for Mexico is who he seems to be—and in the end Randolph Scott gets the girl.

Ronald Reagan and Errol Flynn, *Santa Fe Trail*, Warner Brothers, 1940 MPTVIMAGES.COM

Santa Fe Trail

1940; directed by Michael Curtiz; written by Robert Buckner; starring Errol Flynn, Ronald Reagan, and Olivia de Havilland

Set just before the outbreak of the Civil War, when the West was just opening and the possibilities for its conquerors were still endless, this movie spins a likeable yarn about the story of the real J.E.B. Stuart and his romance with fictional Kit Carson Holliday, and his friendship with George Armstrong Custer.

The seventh Flynn–de Havilland collaboration, the movie has pretty much nothing to do with the Santa Fe Trail or indeed with anything that really happened to all of the characters included in the film, but with Errol Flynn as Stuart, Olivia de Havilland as Kit Carson Holliday, and Ronald Reagan as George Armstrong Custer, it stands alone as pure entertainment. It was wildly popular at the box office in 1940, and while to the modern audience it may seem overly racist, it also does a good job of showing how protagonists on both sides of the Civil War, such as Flynn's J.E.B. Stuart and Reagan's Custer, seem unable to conceive how the issue of slavery could place them on either side of the great Civil War—perhaps the most accurate part of the movie.

The Paleface

1948; directed by Norman Z. McLeod; written by Edmund L. Hartmann and Frank Tashlin; starring Bob Hope and Jane Russell

There are movies that are comedies and there are movies that are Westerns—and there are movies that are both. Rarely has there been a Western comedy as successful as *The Paleface*, starring Bob Hope as Peter Potter, a fish-out-of-water, greenhorn, innocent dupe who ends up marrying Calamity Jane (Jane Russell—the real Calamity Jane would have been delighted) as a part of a plan to keep her identity as a secret agent undercover as she tries to ferret out who is responsible for the gun trafficking that is going on.

Ludicrous? Yes. But delightfully so. When Hope and Russell's wagon train is attacked by the Indians, it's Jane's sharpshooting that saves the day, but she gives the credit to Potter, making the reluctant dentist an instant hero. In the film, Hope sings the song "Buttons and Bows," which became his greatest hit by far when it came to record sales. The song also won the Academy Award for Best Song that year.

Bob Hope gets plaque on Hill COURTESY LIBRARY OF CONGRESS

Angel and the Badman

1947; directed by James Edward Grant; written by James Edward Grant; starring John Wayne, Gail Russell, and Harry Carey

John Wayne smolders as Quirt Evans, an all-round bad guy and womanizer who is wounded and then is nursed back to health and sought after by a Quaker girl named Penelope Worth. Evans falls for Penelope and begins to assimilate her pacifist lifestyle. However, the tug of his old ways is very strong and so he vacillates back and forth. He is finally forced to examine his character after his violent actions bring harm to an innocent person. Eventually, he will find himself having to choose between his world and Penelope's world in a deep look at the ability of a badman to renounce his violent ways. Is it even possible?

The first movie that John Wayne both produced and starred in, this movie was a departure from standard Western fare in its day, and the concept still resonates with moviegoers not just as a Western—its themes were explored again in 1985's *Witness* (Harrison Ford) and 2003's *The Outsider* (Naomi Watts).

Harry Carey, John Wayne, and Gail Russell, *Angel and the Badman*, Republic, 1947 MPTVIMAGES.COM

Duel in the Sun

1946; directed by King Vidor; written by David O. Selznick, Oliver H. P. Garrett, and Ben Hecht, based on a novel by Niven Busch; starring Gregory Peck, Joseph Cotten, and Jennifer Jones

When it came out in 1946, *Duel in the Sun* was described as a *Gone With the Wind*–type epic Western—and as Joseph Cotton drives the wagon carrying beautiful half-breed Pearl Chavez to his family's home against the background of the Technicolor sky, you almost see the ghosts of Rhett, Scarlett, and the retreating southern army just before Rhett leaves her to join the lost cause. Producer David O. Selznick had high hopes that the movie would achieve the greatness of the Civil War epic—and in spite of disappointing critical reviews, it performed very well at the box office. And it was nominated for Academy Awards for Best Actress in a Leading Role (Jennifer Jones) and Best Actress in a Supporting Role (Lillian Gish).

At its heart, the story takes on the age-old themes of sibling rivalry and the relationship between father and son. Torn between her affections for the good son Jesse (Joseph Cotton) and the bad son Lewt (Gregory Peck) of cattle baron Senator Jackson McCanles (played in glorious curmudgeonly style by Lionel Barrymore), Pearl is also caught up in the prejudice of the time and the region. In addition to the rest of the great cast, Lillian Gish is stunning as the matriarch of the family, Laura Belle—the lost love of Pearl's father.

Joseph Cotton and Jennifer Jones, *Duel in the Sun,* The Selznick Studio, 1946 MPTVIMAGES.COM

✳ INVASION OF THE ✳

FANTASY WESTERNS

BY JESSE MULLINS JR. FOR *AMERICAN COWBOY*

Like the Four Horsemen of the Apocalypse, those shadowy apparitions destined to some-day thunder out of nowhere into a world quite unprepared for their assault, so approaches a hard-charging herd of Westerns in full-on, full-tilt fantasy mode. And yet nary a lookout has fired a warning shot, much less circled the wag-ons. Unsuspecting Western traditionalists and purists are sure to be agog as the theaters are lit up with zombie-blasting, alien-stomping, wrangler-zapping, abomination-lassoing action, as howling hordes of frontier combatants decide who really rules the West.

What set off this storm of genre-mashup mayhem? Who the heck knows, but all of Hol-lywood has gotten the memo.

Jonah Hex offers a live-action film version of the DC comic book of the same name. The IMDbPro website describes it this way: "In the Wild West, a scarred bounty hunter tracks a voo-doo practitioner bent on liberating the South by raising an army of the undead."

Death Keeps Coming is a "supernatural Western about an unspeakable horror that arises in the frontier and . . . a mysterious lone gunfighter who tries to save a victim of a horrific gypsy curse."

And then there's *Cowboys & Aliens,* which is set in the 1800s Southwest and is about cowboys banding with Native Americans to fight space aliens that have landed on Earth with plans to enslave humanity.

Meanwhile, *Caliber: First Canon of Justice* turns the Arthurian legend into Old West action, with a tattooed six-gun occupying the place of the Excalibur sword of Arthur's day. This cowboy

Arthur finds his place as a justice-bringer who is the only one who can fire the supernatural weapon, which "never misses."

No sacred cows, or sacred cowboys, are left un-fantasized in this trend, as is shown by the fact that even the forthcoming feature film *The Lone Ranger* is supposed to have "supernatural elements."

How will these pictures sit with the Western-watching public? And what impact will these Westerns—some would likely not call them "Westerns"—have on the long-hoped-for resurrection of the now-moribund genre?

Doubtless, some observers will feel that this development bodes well—that even if die-hard Western fans do not care for the fantasy elements, the mere inclusion of cowboy and Western subject matter could introduce a new generation of viewers to the Western. After all, today's young people have cut their teeth on fantasy video games and fantasy entertainment in general. The idea then would be that, after these viewers' taste is (possibly) whetted by

DVPODT SHUTTERSTOCK

these offerings, they could someday develop a taste for the "real thing"—that is, realistic, traditional Westerns.

Conversely, it's not hard to imagine a crowd that will denounce these intruders as something downright unholy . . . or a laughable folly.

How the West Was Won

1962; directed by John Ford, Henry Hathaway, and George Marshall; written by James R. Webb; starring Henry Fonda, James Stewart, and many, many others

A family saga covering several decades of westward expansion in the nineteenth century, *How the West Was Won* was one of the last "old-fashioned" epic films made by Metro-Goldwyn-Mayer to enjoy great success. It follows four generations of a family as they move ever westward, from western New York state to the Pacific Ocean.

The movie consists of five segments: "The Rivers," "The Plains," "The Outlaws," "The Civil War," and "The Railroad," each taking a piece of the epic of Western expansion and looking at it through the lens of one western-moving family. Three of the segments were directed by Henry Hathaway ("The Rivers," "The Plains," and "The Outlaws"), and one each by John Ford ("The Civil War") and George Marshall ("The Railroad"). The all-star cast includes Carroll Baker, Walter Brennan, Lee J. Cobb, Andy Devine, Henry Fonda, Carolyn Jones, Karl Malden, Harry Morgan, Gregory Peck, George Peppard, Robert Preston, Debbie Reynolds, James Stewart, Eli Wallach, John Wayne, and Richard Widmark. The film is narrated by Spencer Tracy.

The film won three Academy Awards, for Best Writing, Story, and Screenplay Written Directly for the Screen; Best Film Editing; and Best Sound. It was also nominated for Best Picture, Best Art Direction, Best Cinematography, Best Costume Design, and Best Music, Score in its eligible categories.

———•·•———

Raymond Massey, the actor most famous for his portrayals of Abraham Lincoln, would make his final on-screen appearance as the sixteenth president in *How the West Was Won*.

———•·•———

James Stewart and Debbie Reynolds, *How the West Was Won*, MGM, 1962

John Wayne and Marguerite Churchill, *The Big Trail*, Twentieth Century Fox, 1930

The Big Trail

1930; directed by Raoul Walsh and Louis R. Loeffler; written by Hal G. Evarts, Raoul Walsh, Marie Boyle, Jack Peabody, and Florence Postal; starring John Wayne and Marguerite Churchill

There are many reasons that the lavish, widescreen production *The Big Trail,* released in 1930, stands the test of time—but perhaps the most important for many Western fans is the twenty-three-year-old actor who plays Breck Coleman, making his first appearance in a leading role: John Wayne.

The eponymous Big Trail is that great route of Western migration—the Oregon Trail—which was the main conduit for settlers heading to the far reaches of the North American continent from the East from the 1840s to the late 1860s when the continental railroad was completed. Breck Coleman has signed on as the guide and escort for a large party of settlers and the gorgeously filmed cross country journey—perfect for the new widescreen format—is the backdrop for a tale of revenge and romance.

Largely due to the expenses of shooting on location and in the widescreen format, the movie wasn't a financial success. When the effects of the Depression were beginning to be felt by the public, studios abandoned the use of widescreen and color in an attempt to decrease costs. And the charismatic Wayne wouldn't return to mainstream Westerns until Stagecoach in 1939.

———◆———

Because only a small number of theaters could play widescreen films in the 1930s, two versions were always filmed simultaneously, one in 35 mm and one in the 70 mm widescreen. That way, the film would be able to be played even in theaters without widescreen capability.

———◆———

Paint Your Wagon

1969; directed by Joshua Logan; written by Paddy Chayefsky and Alan Jay Lerner; starring Clint Eastwood and Lee Marvin

The premise behind this classic 1969 Western movie musical is fairly absurd. It's the California gold rush, and a farmer from the Midwest and a prospector form an unconventional and unexpected partnership with the end result that they turn their mining camp into a regular boomtown. Among other misadventures, the two "heroes," played by Lee Marvin and Clint Eastwood, buy and share a wife, hijack a stagecoach, and kidnap half a dozen prostitutes. They drink, they sing about the name of the wind ("Mariah"), and they mine for gold. But it's arguably true that there is hardly a more entertaining and enjoyable moment in cinema than Clint Eastwood singing, "I talk to the trees, but they never listen to me." This one makes it into the top one hundred for the sheer fun, exuberance, and zaniness that

happens when one takes a classic Western and adds song and dance—and a truly unexpected, but inspired, cast.

The movie was adapted from the 1951 stage musical by Lerner and Loewe, though there were major changes made to the storyline for the film. Some songs from the original musical were dropped and some were added by Andre Previn, while others were used in different contexts. Eastwood and Marvin did their own singing in the movie.

———•·•———

In 1998, The Simpsons did a tribute to the movie in the episode "All Singing, All Dancing."

———•·•———

Clint Eastwood and Lee Marvin, *Paint Your Wagon*, Paramount Pictures,
1969 MPTVIMAGES.COM

Tombstone

1993; directed by George P. Cosmatos and Kurt Russell; written by Kevin Jarre; starring Kurt Russell and Val Kilmer

This entry in the filmography of the shootout at the O.K. Corral was very successful in theaters when it was released in 1993, earning *Tombstone* $56 million on a $25 million budget. The movie seemed to prove that the moviegoing public still had a taste for the Western. With Kurt Russell as Wyatt Earp, Val Kilmer as the tubercular Doc Holliday, and a huge ensemble cast, the simple plot of a retired lawman looking for a peaceful life and facing his own demons—plus some real ones in the shape of the Clantons—is a formula that proves its worth again.

While this version of the events at Tombstone also takes liberties with the historical record, as epic storytelling it works beautifully. But in the end, Wyatt Earp mostly gets his man and the girl—and Val Kilmer dies with his boots off—tweaking the happy ending. *Tombstone* was released just six months prior to a Kevin Costner movie on Wyatt Earp.

Hearts of the West

1975; directed by Howard Zieff; written by Rob Thompson; starring Jeff Bridges, Andy Griffith, and Blythe Danner

Andy Griffith is the bad guy, Blythe Danner is the ingénue, and Jeff Bridges is the bumbling tenderfoot who dreams of being a cowboy or at least a dime novel writer—what could be better? How about a plot that takes on the genre of the Western B-movie, making a general spoof of the actors, the heroes they portray, and the myth of the Wild West?

Jeff Bridges plays Lewis Tater, a writer who has moved west to follow his dream of writing about the mythical West. Caught up in a bizarre comedy of errors, Tater becomes an accidental B-movie star when he stumbles upon a set while escaping from a couple of bumbling crooks with all of their loot. And in the kind of plot that only happens in Hollywood, Tater becomes a major rival of his favorite film star, played to perfection by Andy Griffith, who, it turns out, isn't really the good guy and paragon of Western virtue he portrays on screen.

A comedy movie that gently and amusingly pokes fun at the foibles of the movies of old—and about Westerns and their largely venerated stars—this find-it-on-VHS classic from the 1970s is worth the effort.

———•———

A postscript to this story is one of those delightful, truth-is-stranger-than-fiction, only-in-Hollywood twists of fate, Jeff Bridges is now one of those venerated Western stars, reprising the great John Wayne's Rooster Cogburn in the Coen brothers' version of *True Grit*.

———•———

Hang 'em High

1968; directed by Ted Post; written by Leonard Freeman, Mel Goldberg; starring Clint Eastwood, Inger Stevens, Ed Begley, and Ben Johnson

After the success of the Sergio Leone Dollars trilogy, Clint Eastwood was a star—and from the moment his character, Jed Cooper, is dragged into the frame under the hanging tree by the mob intending to lynch him, he proves that stardom is well earned. The first movie produced by the Malpaso Company, which was Clint Eastwood's own production company, is a classic tale of revenge and personal conscience with a heady mix of danger and excitement. The story is set in Oklahoma Territory in 1889. When Cooper survives the attempted lynching, he takes on the very personal responsibility of bringing the vigilantes to justice—unfortunately choosing their kind of justice before turning his ways around.

Through the twists and turns of the plot, viewers are introduced to characters like Judge Adam Fenton, who may be based on a real-life "hanging judge" of the late nineteenth century; the U.S. Marshal charged with rounding up criminals for the judge (Ben Johnson); the town lunatic (memorably executed in a short scene by Dennis Hopper); and the beautiful storekeeper (Inger Stevens).

A major financial success, *Hang 'Em High* even exceeded the one-day revenue of the James Bond franchise to that time. It also solidified Clint Eastwood as a presence on the big screen—a presence that has lasted more than four decades.

Shadow of the noose VALENTIN AGAPOV, SHUTTERSTOCK

Ten Wanted Men

1955; directed by H. Bruce Humberstone; written by Kenneth Gamet, based on the story by Irving Ravetch; starring Randolph Scott, Jocelyn Brando, and Richard Boone

Randolph Scott was a prolific actor, appearing in more than one hundred films during his career—but he is most associated with the classic, tall-in-the-saddle Western hero (though he did play a villain now and then). Some critics prefer Scott's work with director Budd Boetticher, which did give him a late-career boost, but unlike the darker, dialogue heavy (though still great) Boetticher movies, this more traditional Western offers intense action, a strong plot, and a fast pace that made it a favorite with audiences in 1955 and helps it stand out in the genre.

In *Ten Wanted Men*, Randolph Scott plays John Stewart, an Arizona rancher who tries to rule over his cattle empire by force of will and with utmost integrity. His foil is the jealous rival rancher Wick Campbell (Richard Boone) who shows what he's made of by rustling cattle, murdering rivals, and bringing in hired guns to act as enforcers. The crux of the movie is the life-or-death choice that Stewart must make in order to save all he loves from destruction by the wicked Campbell.

Nineteen-year-old George Randolph Scott enlisted in the Army in 1917 and served in France as an artillery observer during World War I before dropping the George from his name and playing a hero on the silver screen.

GUNFIGHTS

BY RON SOODALTER

Two men stand crouched at opposite ends of a dusty street; hands poised claw-like over low-slung, tied-down Colts. Slowly they walk towards each other. They stop, waiting as the music builds to a crescendo, and, as if at some unseen signal, they draw. Their speed is stunning—one man spins and goes down, killed by a single, well-placed shot, while the other stands immobile for a moment, unchanged but for a sad, wistful expression that crosses his face like a cloud. He sighs, holsters his pistol with an unconsciously flashy twirl, and walks away. The morality play is over. Good has triumphed over evil. Again. And forever, all the way back to the earliest days of the Western. It was, to those of us of a certain age, our most indelible lesson in the story of the winning of the West. And, as with so much of our nation's history that we were fed both in and out of school, the image is almost completely false.

The handgun used in Hollywood Westerns is nearly always the Colt Model 1873 Single Action Army revolver. While the popularity of that model is undeniable, there were a wide variety of weapons employed back in the day. James B. "Killin' Jim" Miller favored a shotgun when on the job. Wyoming range detective Tom Horn carried a Colt .45 model 1878 double action. Some preferred "thumb-busters," while others leaned toward double actions. And many supplemented their arsenals with stingy—or hideaway, or belly—guns. Commonly, however, men who relied on firepower—while perhaps leaning towards a specific model—owned and used a variety of weapons.

As to how they stowed their "hoglegs," Hollywood is again far from the mark. Although modern Westerns are paying attention to period accuracy, the earliest movies tended to feature the most accurate gun leather, for the simple reason that the prop departments owned the original rigs. They weren't that old back then! For this reason, I love the William S. Hart silents—great outfits, great rigs.

The original civilian holsters, from the days of the Colt Paterson into the 1870s, were narrow, somewhat tubular affairs referred to as "Slim Jims." Starting around the mid-1870s, holsters made in what is often called the "Mexican loop" style—with a single piece of leather folding back on itself to form a skirt through which the belt passed—became popular. This was the holster that saw the most frequent use. And belt pistols were worn high on the hip. Practically no one wore his gun low and tied down—it was simply inconvenient.

By the 1930s, Hollywood Westerns favored a "buscadero" rig, a modern design that features a low-slung holster. Versions worn by the celluloid heroes were often heavily studded, silver mounted, and totally removed from the utilitarian holsters worn in the nineteenth century.

In the 1950s, a quick-draw artist and entrepreneur named Arvo Ojala modified the basic buscadero rig to design a holster that exposed the entire trigger guard, hammer, and part of the cylinder. He also lined the pouch with steel, so that the cylinder could turn freely before leaving the holster. In this way, the gun could be drawn and cocked in a single motion. It made for a low-cut, low-hung holster that was impractical for anything besides the rapid extraction of a pistol, but it fulfilled that function admirably. It also took us one step further away from historical accuracy.

By 1960, Westerns were the biggest thing on television, with more than two-dozen oaters running every week. And in their bid for the ratings, they all seemed to have a gun-related gimmick. Don Durant as "Johnny Ringo" carried a LeMat revolver, with that lethal shotgun charge. Earl Holliman's Sundance Kid, in the one-season wonder *Hotel de Paree*, wore a hatband of silver conchos that blinded his opponent (not very sporting, but effective). "The Rifleman" had a modified '92 Winchester that could put them all in the center or ignite a row of matches when quick-fired from the thigh. And don't get me started on *The Wild, Wild West*.

Matt Dillon (of *Gunsmoke*), admirable character though he was, wasn't really that fast. Neither was Paladin, although it was a great show. All the Warner Brothers Western leads (and the list seemed endless) practiced with their fast draw rigs—it must have been a provision in their contracts—and a number of them, including John Russell, Peter Brown, Clint Walker, Ty Hardin, and James Garner, became quite proficient. But the fastest of them all was Pat Conway, who starred as Marshal Clay Hollister in a short-lived series called *Tombstone Territory*. Forgettable show; incredible draw.

Europe picked up on the quick-draw theme, and beginning with the spaghetti Westerns of the 1960s, had a field day offering up variations of the scruffy "antihero" whose redeeming skill was the ability to outdraw and kill at least three men at a time. The Roy and Gene days of "winging" your opponent were over. It was all about body count, and these guys meant business.

Generally, gunfighting in the Old West was more an occasional occurrence than a regular event. It's just more exciting to make movies about pistoleros than storekeepers—unless, like Fred MacMurray and Glenn Ford, they're storekeepers who take up a gun in the last ten minutes of the film. And far from being battles between the forces of light and darkness, real gunfights were often just quarrels that had gotten past the point of verbal resolution. The concept of good versus evil usually had nothing to do with it.

And while a gunfighter's success depends largely on the proficient use of his weapons, the blinding speed of today's quick-draw artists would not have been much of a consideration in the Old West. In their last moments, most of our enduring real-life Western icons would have had no need for a fast draw, since they never saw death coming.

Let's look at the record: Jesse James was shot in the back of the head, as were John Wesley Hardin, Bill Hickok, and Dallas Stoudenmire. Pat Garrett shot an almost certainly unarmed Billy the Kid from hiding, in a dark room, and was himself assassinated while urinating. Morgan Earp was shot in the back while shooting billiards, and Ben Thompson and King Fisher were shot from above, with no chance to draw their weapons. Jim Miller shot his victims from ambush, as did some of the "regulators" who were paid to resolve stock wars or personal feuds. And in the instances in which men actually did face each other, very rarely was the swiftness of the draw an issue. (An exception was Hickok, whose speed and accuracy, though doubtless enhanced with the passing of years, was acknowledged even in his own time.) There is an inherently brutal logic at work here: If you resent and fear a man enough to kill him, the last thing you want to do is give him an even break. Most real gunfights were not equal opportunity events.

Consider the Mather-Nixon fight. In 1884, "Mysterious" Dave Mather owned a saloon in

Dodge City, and became embroiled in a quarrel with Tom Nixon, an early-day pioneer and rival saloon owner. In an attempt to resolve the disagreement quickly, Nixon made two mistakes—he fired at Mather, and he missed. Nixon was arrested on charges of attempted murder, but ominously, Mather declined to press charges. Shortly thereafter, he walked up behind Nixon and, without preamble, placed several bullets in him. Mather was arrested on murder charges—and acquitted on grounds of self-defense. If Mather hadn't stopped Nixon's clock when he did, the jury reasoned, sooner or later Nixon would have killed him.

One thing is clear from this story, aside from the jury's lenient interpretation of the law: You didn't just walk away from gunplay, the movies notwithstanding. If you shot a man, or sometimes if you simply shot at a man, you would be arrested and, in all likelihood, tried. The O.K. Corral altercation, for example, was only the beginning of the Earps' troubles. They and Doc Holliday were arrested, charged, and tried for murder.

One of my favorite gunfights took place in Dodge City's elegant Long Branch Saloon, in the spring of 1879. It occurred between two adversaries: Levi Richardson, a beefy teamster and buffalo hunter, and "Cockeyed Frank" Loving, a young cowboy-turned-gambler. The Long Branch was crowded on the night of April 5, when Richardson entered, bought a drink, sat at Loving's table, and began to berate him. The two traded insults and Richardson drew his pistol. Loving followed suit, and they chased each other first around a potbellied stove, and then around a billiards table, firing repeatedly and at such close range that Richardson's coat caught fire. Patrons headed for whatever exits and cover they could find, one man climbing into the ice chest. By the time City Marshal Charlie Bassett came in and broke up the fight, Loving's pistol was empty, and Richardson's had just one remaining load. Loving had only a minor scratch on his hand, but Richardson had received a mortal wound to the chest. Incredibly, no one else was shot. One wonders what Hollywood would have made of a gunfight in which a man fires five rounds point blank, and succeeds in merely scratching his opponent's hand.

Loving reportedly joked often with his friends that "it was his slow draw that enabled him to come out the winner." The killing was ruled a justifiable homicide, and "Cockeyed Frank" soon left Dodge for Trinidad, Colorado, where he promptly ran afoul of another gambler named John Allen. In the fight that ensued, the two men chased each other through the various rooms of the local saloon (Loving's fights apparently involved a lot of leg work), emptying and reloading their pistols without effect, until Loving ducked into a nearby hardware store to reload yet again. Allen sneaked in through the basement and up the stairs, and fatally shot Loving in the back. Loving immediately identified Allen as his killer, and the marshal arrested him in the stairway just steps from where Loving was shot. A twenty-man guard was posted around Allen to prevent a lynching, and on Loving's death a week later, he was tried for murder—and acquitted. Allen traveled to Dodge, where he became a preacher, and, in the words of Bat Masterson, "of course, all was forgiven."

Even allowing for some embellishment over the years as fact entered the realm of folklore, stories such as these are remarkable, as much for the part played by circumstance as for the grit shown by the players. But they are far from what has been called the "classic Western shoot-out"—the clearly defined one-act play that was made formulaic over decades of celluloid Westerns—composed of the walk-down, the quick draw, and the villain dying in the dirt street, often gasping some last words for dramatic closure.

All of this raises the question, "Does Hollywood ever get it right?" The answer: occasionally, but not often. I was fourteen when a series debuted called *Westerner,* starring Brian Keith as an itinerant cowboy named Dave Blassingame

and directed by a young Sam Peckinpah. It was a wonderfully gritty, often believable series with no slick gimmicks, which is probably why it lasted only one season. One episode struck me then, and has stayed with me ever since. It co-starred Ben Cooper as a gun-crazy young Eastern transplant, and Michael Ansara as a seasoned Mexican cowboy. Cooper goads Ansara through most of the show's half hour, until, sitting in a saloon, a disgusted Keith shows the kid a pistol cartridge, explaining, "That's a .45 caliber, 240-grain hunk of lead that can splatter your brains like a jumped-on squash." He asks if the youth has ever seen a bullet hole up close: "Oh, it goes in little enough," Keith explains. "But then it tears you up inside and when it comes out—that's if you're lucky and it comes out—it leaves a hole about like that," he says, holding up his fist.

Keith tells Ansara to show Cooper what kind of damage a .45 slug can do. Reluctantly, Ansara lifts his shirt, showing exactly the kind of wound Keith has just described—small in front, and massive and scarred in back. The young Cooper is not discouraged, and pushing Ansara to the point of no return, he goes into the street to wait. As soon as Ansara walks through the saloon doors, Cooper quick-draws, and rapid-fires five shots—missing every time. Meanwhile Ansara slowly draws, extends his arm, aims,

and fires a single kill shot into Cooper. Ansara holsters his pistol and walks away past the kid's prone form without a downward glance.

No cinematic description of a gunfight has ever rivaled the story Little Bill Daggett tells the writer Beauchamp in *Unforgiven*. His first-hand account of how English Bob slew "Two-Gun" Corcoran is classic. He takes a story that has already gone through the legend-making process, and reduces it to what it was: a drunken altercation over a whore, in which fair play had no part ("Before he knows what's happening, Bob here takes a shot at him!"), marksmanship was poor ("because he's so damned drunk"), and luck played a vital role ("The Walker Colt blew up in his hand—which was a failing common to that model."). It doesn't get any better.

Most recently, the movie *Appaloosa*, based on Robert B. Parker's novel, features pistol fights that have the ring of authenticity. In one instance, the characters approach each other with guns drawn, and commence shooting as soon as they are within range. There are six men firing, and within seconds, five are down and one runs away. One of the characters comments on how quickly it ended, to which another replies, "Everybody could shoot."

Rarely in movies does a pistol sound or kick the way it should. Again, *Appaloosa* is an exception; the short, loud, staccato "pop" of a large-bore pistol is unmistakable. So, too, in the underrated Charlton Heston vehicle, *Will Penny*. When Lee Majors fires his sheriff's model .45, it bucks every time. And in 1992's *Tombstone*, the pistols and shotguns recoil consistently and realistically. It might seem a trivial point to many, but to us purists, the more credible the historical details, the likelier it is that we will suspend our disbelief and buy into the story. I'm still waiting for a cinematic shootout in which black powder smoke fills the room after a serious exchange of gunfire.

After all the comparisons and analyses, there is the irony that my generation grew up on Hollywood's tried-and-true version of the gunfighter—only to become its harshest critics. Yet, without *Gunsmoke, Have Gun–Will Travel, Wanted: Dead or Alive,* or even *Sugarfoot,* we wouldn't have pestered our parents into buying us those Mattel Fanner 50s or Nichols Stallion .45s. We wouldn't have practiced constantly in front of the mirror, or tested our speed, day in and day out, against our friends down the street. In short, we wouldn't have developed our somewhat healthy obsession with the Old West, and most specifically with its shootists. In the end, they really are more interesting than storekeepers.

The Virginian

1929; directed by Victor Fleming; written by Howard Estabrook and Grover Jones; starring Gary Cooper, Walter Huston, and Richard Arlen

Ten years before he tackled the classic novels *The Wizard of Oz* and *Gone With the Wind*, director Victor Fleming turned his attention to the great classic Western that started it all, filming *The Virginian* with Gary Cooper, Walter Huston, and Richard Arlen.

The novel (and stage play) set many of the formulas that have characterized almost every Western since—whether by directors following those formulas or turning them on their heads. And as a movie, *The Virginian* stands the test of time, having started many of those conventions.

In the movie, the Virginian (Gary Cooper) runs afoul of a bunch of outlaws who are rustling his cattle. After catching some of them, he organizes their lynching—but the leader of the gang, Trampas (Walter Huston) manages to escape justice.

Eventually, the Virginian meets Trampas in a shootout on a dusty Western street and metes out that justice in one of the great shootouts ever captured on film. But movie is probably most famous for the poker scene, in which the Virginian responds to Trampas's "You long-legged sonova—."

"If you wanna call me that, smile."

The Virginian by Owen Wister and Kirke La Shelle, theatrical poster from 1903

Lone Star

1996; directed by John Sayles; written by John Sayles; starring Stephen Mendillio, Stephen J. Lang, and Chris Cooper

A Western and a murder mystery, John Sayles' *Lone Star* manages to succeed heartily on both fronts by introducing a landscape and characters and themes that are key to a successful Western, as well as dipping a toe into the waters of racial prejudice and politics that have taken many a great Western to the next level. He ups the ante with the story of Sheriff Sam Deeds's quest to find out who murdered the old sheriff forty years earlier, burying him in the desert—and who his father, the legendary "Buddy" Deeds, really was.

There are enough twists and turns in this movie to satisfy a roller coaster enthusiast, and the surprises that are revealed as the truth comes to light made this one of the most talked-about movies of 1996. Tightly woven plot lines and brilliantly executed and complex characters, along with a very satisfactory use of flashbacks, have kept this movie in the top one hundred for more than ten years and we expect it will remain there.

Run of the Arrow

1957; directed by Samuel Fuller; written by Samuel Fuller; starring Rod Stieger, Sara Montiel, Brian Keith, and Charles Bronson

In one of the earliest movie appearances in the great Rod Stieger's legendary career, he plays a Confederate veteran named O'Meara who, after Lee's surrender at Appomatox Courthouse, refuses to surrender himself. He makes his way West where he marries a Sioux woman and lives among the tribe—having to choose between his adopted people and his renounced homeland as the movie unfolds.

Run of the Arrow is one of those movies that is virtually unknown by audiences today—but definitely worth tracking down.

The Vanishing American

1926; directed by George B. Seitz; written by Ethel Doherty, based on the novel by Zane Grey; starring Richard Dix, Lois Wilson, and Noah Beery

Can a silent movie, released in theaters in 1926, be considered "revisionist?" Notable for its sympathetic treatment of Native Americans and moral caution, this movie certainly would seem to fall into that category of Westerns that gained a foothold in the latter half of the twentieth century. As this movie, which is based on the Zane Grey novel, unfolds, Indians in Monument Valley, Utah, wipe out the ancient cliff dwellers only to face the same defeat by the European settlers who move in. On the Navajo reservation in the early twentieth century, the Indian-hating Booker is the overseer who is stealing horses from them for profit. When World War I starts, an Army captain comes west to investigate where the horses are going—they're needed in the war effort.

A strong denunciation of the exploitation and oppression of Native Americans, but not an overly romantic view of the American West, this is a movie that asks the big questions that are an undercurrent in human interactions today. In the movie, the Native Americans end up serving as soldiers in World War I, only to return to the dire situation on the reservation. This is a great movie to watch as a counterpoint to a lot of the other early Westerns—as interesting a glimpse into the 1920s as it is into the culture of the West.

✖ HOLLYWOOD-WORTHY HEROICS ✖

KEN AMOROSANO FOR *AMERICAN COWBOY* MAGAZINE

Very rarely do real-life gunfights live up to the Hollywood ideal, but there were a few that defied all odds and logic to see a single man prevail against overwhelming numbers.

During the 1878–79 Lincoln County War, Dick Brewer and his band of fourteen or so Regulators tried to arrest a cantankerous old member of the Murphy-Dolan faction named Andrew "Buckshot" Roberts. When told to surrender, Roberts responded, "Not much, MaryAnn," and brought his Winchester, "Old Betsy," to bear. Roberts had a crippled arm from an earlier engagement. Nonetheless, he managed to kill Brewer, wound three others, and put another out of commission with a shot to the belt buckle. Roberts himself took a mortal wound to the stomach, and the Regulators elected to let the old he-wolf die on his own rather than continue to face his fire.

In 1884, a brash New Mexican teenager named Elfego Baca declared himself a law officer and proceeded to arrest a drunken cowboy. According to the legend, the cowboy's eighty companions—all members of John Slaughter's tough Texas crew—took offense and besieged Baca for a day and a half, allegedly firing some 4,000 rounds into the house where he had taken refuge. Baca miraculously emerged from the house untouched and during the fight reportedly managed to kill four of the Texans and wound eight more. Baca was acquitted after the door of the house—showing some 400 bullet holes—was introduced as evidence. He left the courthouse and embarked on a long career in law enforcement.

In 1892, a consortium of big Wyoming cattlemen imported an army of Texas gunmen and invaded Johnson County with orders to kill the small ranchers and "rustlers." Their first target was a tough cowboy named Nate Champion. From dawn till late in the afternoon, fifty men fired into Nate's cabin without effect, while Champion fired back and—with incredible presence of mind—kept a journal of his last day. In desperation, the attackers set fire to the cabin and shot Nate to doll rags when he made his break. But his last stand gave the small ranchers and townspeople of Johnson County the time to mount a counterattack and stop the invasion cold.

The Outlaw Josey Wales

1976; directed by Clint Eastwood; written by Philip Kaufman and Sonia Chernus, based on the book *Gone to Texas* by Forrest Carter; starring Clint Eastwood and Sondra Locke

Directed by and starring Clint Eastwood as Josey Wales, this movie, based on the book *Gone to Texas* by Forrest Carter, finds its place in the top one hundred for its gutsy portrayals of the shades of gray between the black hats and the white hats of the heroes and villains populating the popular Western genre, reversing the movie stereotypes of Union and Confederate soldiers that had predominated up to that time in film.

Josey Wales is a Missouri farmer who joins up with a guerrilla unit of Confederates after Union soldiers murder his family. At the end of the war, most of the guerrillas are persuaded to surrender, but not Josey Wales, who begins a life on the run, heading for what he hopes is a new beginning in Texas.

The role of Josey Wales is iconic—as is the atmosphere created by the movie. It received an Academy Award nomination, it was a critical and commercial success, and in 1994, the National Film Registry of the Library of Congress selected it for inclusion and preservation.

———

The Outlaw Josey Wales was inspired by a 1972 novel by an American-Indian writer named Forrest Carter, originally titled *Gone to Texas* and later retitled *The Rebel Outlaw: Josey Wales,* except that it would be revealed that the real author was Asa Carter, a one-time racist and supporter of the Ku Klux Klan.

———

Sandra Locke, Clint Eastwood, and extras, *The Outlaw Josey Wales,* Warner Brothers, 1976 MPTVIMAGES.COM

Jeremiah Johnson

1972; directed by Sydney Pollack; written by Raymond W. Thorp, based on the novel by Vardis Fisher; starring Robert Redford, Will Gere, and Delle Bolton

Released in 1972 and starring Robert Redford as the eponymous Jeremiah Johnson, this Sydney Pollock classic is notable for its gorgeous scenery but also for its thoughtful interpretation of the genre and of the Western experience. It's a movie of its era about another time—the former soldier comes home and adopts the life of a hermit, only to be thrust into another war, this time as the subject of a vendetta started by an accidental intrusion into an Indian burial ground.

Loosely based on the legend/true story of John Johnston, who changed his name to John Johnson and later became known as "Liver-Eatin" Johnson, this is a great movie about a lone man facing the wilderness, unexpectedly finding himself less alone than he intended, and facing off against his demons. But it's also a movie about how legends and myths grow.

Robert Redford, *Jeremiah Johnson,* Warner Brothers, 1972 MPTVIMAGES.COM

Cowboy

1958; directed by Delmer Daves; written by Edmund H. North, based on the book by Frank Harris; starring Glenn Ford, Jack Lemmon, and Anna Kashfi

Frank Harris (Jack Lemmon), a Chicago hotel clerk with a dream of the West, thwarted in love by the father of the object of his affections, joins a cattle drive headed up by Tom Reese (Glenn Ford).

In classic, tenderfoot-out-of-water tradition, the life he's expected to live on the range doesn't live up to his expectations. The whole story is based on a brief excerpt from the real Frank Harris's autobiography about his turn with a cattle rustler (Hollywood of the late 1950s still liked its heroes on the right side of the law).

Brian Donlevy plays a former town marshal who joins the drive to get away from his job, and Jack Lemmon's casting in the Frank Harris role makes one think a bit of *City Slickers*—but this is a realistic cattle drive, which is the problem for Harris, who's gotten all of his expectations from dime novels.

———•·•———

Yes, that's Dick York, Darren of *Bewitched,* as Charlie the trail hand.

———•·•———

Barbarosa

1982; directed by Fred Schepisi; written by William D. Wittliff; starring Willie Nelson, Gary Busey, and Isela Vega

After Karl Westover (Gary Busey), a farm boy in pre–Civil War Texas, accidentally kills his brother-in-law, he flees toward Mexico and on his way meets up with the outlaw Barbarosa (Willie Nelson), who befriends the boy but encourages him to go home before making his way to his next crime scene. Naturally, Karl doesn't go home, and he and Barbarosa meet again when the outlaw robs the cantina Karl is in at gunpoint. The two form an unlikely partnership and Karl learns the ways of the outlaw while being pursued by the brothers of the man he killed in Texas. Barbarosa is also in danger from a vengeful family—his father-in-law has vowed to kill him for marrying his daughter without permission.

This was one of the most underrated movies of the 1980s, but the performances by Gary Busey and Willie Nelson were nonetheless terrific, the story is fast paced and well plotted, and the supporting cast contributes beautifully to the humor and the drama. It has developed somewhat of a cult following in the ensuing decades and rightfully earns top one hundred mention.

One-Eyed Jacks

1961; directed by Marlon Brando; written by Guy Trosper and Calder Willingham; starring Marlon Brando, Karl Malden, Katy Jurado, and Ben Johnson

Marlon Brando directed and starred in this 1961 Western about an outlaw who double-crosses his partner when they're on the run from the law after a bank robbery in Mexico and the aftermath of that betrayal. Karl Malden even claimed that Marlon Brando was mostly responsible for writing the story for the film, which was very loosely based on the novel *The Authentic Death of Hendry Jones* by Charles Neider.

Brando is Rio who, along with his partner Dad Longworth (Karl Malden), has made away with a fortune in stolen gold. Longworth takes the gold, leaving Rio to be captured, and years later Rio escapes from prison looking for Longworth and seeking revenge. Amazingly, Longworth has become the sheriff of Monterey, California, where Rio plans a bank robbery, falls in love with Longworth's stepdaughter, plots and rejects revenge plans, and is eventually arrested again for a robbery he didn't commit. And there are more twists to the story to come.

———•••———

One-Eyed Jacks was the name of a brothel in the television series *Twin Peaks*. In the show Audrey asks Donna if she has heard of One-Eyed Jacks, and Donna responds, "Isn't that that Western with Marlon Brando?"

———•••———

Bad Company

1972; directed by Robert Benton; written by David Newman and Robert Benton; starring Jeff Bridges, Barry Brown, and Jim Davis

Set during the Civil War, *Bad Company* follows the career of a young boy named Drew Dixon (Barry Brown) who has run away to avoid service in the Union army and heads west with only a gold watch and $100 to his name. His goal is to reach Virginia City, in Nevada Territory, but along the way he's robbed by a con artist and thief named Jake Rumsey (Jeff Bridges) in St. Joseph, Missouri. Later he joins Jake's gang of ragtag young men heading West for a life of freedom from civilization that comes with a higher price than any of them is prepared to pay.

Jeff Bridges's Jake Rumsey is an Artful Dodger type who manages to convey mischief through his malice. His work, and Barry Brown's Drew Dixon, brought life to a movie that was filled with authentic period detail, humor, violence, and adventure. Though it received mixed reviews when it came out, it has definitely held up and gained in reputation through the decades. Some viewers and critics think it's Robert Benton's best movie—and he later directed *The Late Show* (1977), *Kramer vs. Kramer* (1979), and *Places in the Heart* (1984).

Ramrod

1947; directed by Andre DeToth; written by Jack Moffitt, based on a story by Luke Short; starring Joel McCrea and Veronica Lake

Walking the fine line between classic Western and the great film noir of its era, and combining the classic cowboy style of Joel McCrea with the sultry noir style of Veronica Lake, this is a movie that uses and then defies stereotypes—a great classic on its own two feet.

Connie Dickason (Veronica Lake) has lost her fiancé in a range war over sheep and cattle ranching, but she's determined to run the ranch herself with the help of recovering alcoholic Dave Nash (McCrea) and a crew that loathes the "boss" of the area, who is determined to take down Dickason through violence, just as she is determined to take down his operation through legal means.

Betrayal and deception on both sides of the range war lead to no one knowing who to trust—the paranoia builds throughout the movie. There's a dark edge to everything that happens on screen, and as the true villains are revealed, viewers will find themselves, cliché or not, on the edge of their seats. Connie Dickason claims that as a woman, she doesn't need guns. It may be true.

Veronica Lake, *Ramrod*, United Artists, 1947 MPTVIMAGES.COM

The Long Riders

1980; directed by Walter Hill; written by Bill Bryden and Steven Smith; starring David Carradine, Keith Carradine, Robert Carradine, James Keach, and Stacy Keach

Walter Hill put together some of the greatest Western casts of the late twentieth century, and in choosing actual brothers to play the James brothers (James and Stacy Keach), the Younger brothers (David, Keith, and Robert Carradine), the Fords (Christopher and Nicholas Guest), and the Millers (Randy and Dennis Quaid) he puts together a group of actors who rise above the gimmick and turn out a terrific movie that puts a sympathetic spin on the story of bank robbers and outlaws forced into their lifestyle by circumstance.

When the movie came out it got huge critical acclaim for its portrayals of the famous legends of the old West and for the action and drama embodied in the film. Themes of loyalty and betrayal work especially well with the sibling relationships and break it out of the "Western" mold, but by golly it's a great Western.

David Carradine, Keith Carradine, Robert Carradine, Randy Quaid, Stacy Keach, and James Keach, *The Long Riders,* 1980,
© 1980 Mel Traxel MPTVIMAGES.COM

The Missing

2003; directed by Ron Howard; written by Ken Kaufman, based on the novel *The Last Ride* by Thomas Eidson; starring Tommy Lee Jones, Cate Blanchett, and Val Kilmer

An uneasy relationship between a father and daughter on the frontier is at the core of this 2003 Ron Howard film—a film that pays tribute to *The Searchers* and strives for realism through the lens of a thriller.

When the eldest daughter of Maggie Jones (Cate Blanchett) is kidnapped by the Apache, in 1885 New Mexico, she's forced to team up with her estranged father, Samuel Jones (Tommy Lee Jones) to rescue her.

Ultimately this ends up being a story of redemption for the father who had abandoned his family.

———•·•———

Actors in *The Missing* spent hours studying the Apache language in order to achieve an authentic use of it in the movie.

———•·•———

Four Faces West

1949; directed by Alfred E. Green; written by C. Graham Baker and Teddi Sherman; starring Joel McCrea, Frances Dea, Charles Bickford, Joseph Calleia, and William Conrad

It's a Western with no real bad guys and a Western without a gunfight. This great Joel McCrea classic tells the story of a bank robbed at gunpoint—in an effort to save the family ranch—and the characters with whom the bank robber comes in contact as he attempts to evade capture by the new U.S. Marshal, Pat Garrett, using his wits and the kindness of strangers.

Joel McCrea plays Ross McEwen, the rancher down on his luck who robs the bank, and his real-life wife Frances Dee plays Fay Hollister, the kindly nurse who tends his wound from a rattlesnake bite as he attempts his escape from Pat Garrett (Charles Bickford).

ANDREAS MEYER SHUTTERSTOCK

The Ballad of Little Jo

1993; directed by Maggie Greenwald; written by Maggie Greenwald; starring Suzy Amis, Bo Hopkins, and Ian McKellen

Josephine Monaghan (Suzy Amis), a young, pretty, privileged woman of the mid-1800s, flees to the West after giving birth to an illegitimate child—and finds out that it's not particularly safe to be young, pretty, privileged, and a woman in that time and that place. So she disguises herself as a young man named Jo and works to survive and live an independent life in a small mining town on the frontier. It's a saga made for the movies and yet based on a true story of a woman who fled her upbringing and made a life for herself in the frontier West, working as a shepherd, and eventually buying her own homestead. And, in the movie, she has an affair with the Chinese man she hires as a cook—who is much smarter than the face he puts on for the world, a survival tactic much like Jo's own.

As the plot develops, the classic Western theme of the feud between sheepmen and cattlemen over the availability of grazing land takes shape and Jo is faced with the choice of going back to life as a woman and selling her property. Ultimately, she stands her ground and it isn't discovered that she is female until after her death years later.

The Covered Wagon

1923; directed by James Cruze; written by Jack Cunningham, based on the novel by Emerson Hough; starring J. Warren Kerrigan, Lois Wilson, and Alan Hale

A love triangle on the Oregon Trail offers the underpinnings for this story's westward progression. After two caravans combine in Kansas City, they head into the great unknown—the desert heat, mountain snow, the privations of the trail, and the ever-present fear of Indian attack. The beautiful young pioneer woman, Molly, must choose between Sam, the former brute, and Will, the dashing caravan leader with a secret in his past.

The Covered Wagon was one of the top grossing films of 1923. It was expensive to produce but after its strong performance at the box office it opened the door for many, many more Westerns in the years that followed.

No Name on the Bullet

1959; directed by Jack Arnold; written by Gene L. Coon, based on the story by Howard Amacker; starring Audie Murphy, Charles Drake, Joan Evans, and Virginia Grey

Supsense and tension, rather than shoot-'em-up action, makes *No Name on the Bullet* one of our top one hundred Westerns of all time. Audie Murphy is brilliant as the cool, collected professional assassin John Gant. And the paranoia that erupts in the little town of Lordsburg, where everyone has an enemy and a guilty conscience, while they wait to find out who he's there to kill makes this a thriller of the first degree.

No one is absolutely certain whom Gant has come to kill and as he bides his time, citizens crack under the pressure.

ORIONTRAIL SHUTTERSTOCK

Brokeback Mountain

2005; directed by Ang Lee; written by Larry McMurtry, based on a short story by E. Annie Proulx; starring Heath Ledger, Jake Gyllenhall, and Randy Quaid

Set in the Big Horn Mountains of Wyoming and based on the story by Annie Proulx, *Brokeback Mountain* was one of the most honored, analyzed, controversial, and ubiquitous movies of 2005.

The story is straightforward enough: two young ranch hands develop a bond during their long months working together alone in the mountains and, after a passionate night together, begin a twenty-year affair that they hide from their families and others around them. But of course it's not simple. When the story begins, its 1963 and they're cowboys.

After leaving Brokeback Mountain, both marry but it's clear that their past and their love for each other will color all of their relationships for the rest of their lives. After Jack is killed, Ennis, who has divorced but lives near his grown children, reveals the depth of his love—at least to himself—but the social mores of the time are an important unnamed character is this drama.

When *Entertainment Weekly* named *Brokeback Mountain* to its best of the decade list they said, "Everyone called it 'The Gay Cowboy Movie.' Until they saw it. In the end, Ang Lee's 2005 love story wasn't gay or straight, just human." But because it was a cowboy movie—and because it looks at an interesting part of the West in an interesting way, it justly deserves a spot on this list, as well.

Including its three Academy Awards (Best Director, Best Adapted Screenplay, and Best Score) and four Golden Globes (Best Motion Picture—Drama, Best Director, Best Song, and Best Screenplay), *Brokeback Mountain* was nominated for 123 major awards and won 71 of them. Despite the controversies surrounding the movie, it earns a place in the top one hundred as a sweeping look at a way of life in a time in history that's recent enough to be remembered and should not be forgotten.

Western Union

1941; directed by Fritz Lang; written by Robert Carson, based on the novel by Zane Grey; starring Robert Young, Randolph Scott, and Dean Jagger

Robert Young is the Harvard engineer and Dean Jagger is the visionary—both dream of putting together a transcontinental telegraph in the early years of the Civil War. And Randolph Scott is the reformed outlaw who is now a member of the team stretching the lines of communication into the West.

Director Fritz Lang was known for his crime films, but this Western gave him a chance to show off his skills and his knowledge of the American West. The period detail is wonderful and the sets and scenery are gorgeous. A forest fire, two skirmishes with Indians, and incursions by Confederate raiders make up the action. But what's nice about this movie is that for all of the standard Western trappings, the heroes aren't just the guys who wear the white hats, and it's a surprise when we find out who gets the girl. Great performances by Randolph Scott, Robert Young, and John Carradine help make this a classic.

From *Harper's Weekly,* Army setting up telegraph lines—art imitating history LIBRARY OF CONGRESS

Support Your Local Sheriff

1969; directed by Burt Kennedy; written by William Bowers; starring James Garner, Walter Brennan, and Harry Morgan

When the tough, competent, and handsome Jason McCullough (James Garner) rides into the Old West town of Calendar from "back East" on his way to Australia, he's the answer to the townsfolks' prayers. Calendar is a town that grew up overnight after a gold strike (the adorably klutzy Prudy Perkins discovered the gold in a grave during a funeral). The free-for-all that followed the strike has turned the town into a drunken festival and a target for the bandits known as the Danbys, who control the only route out of town and thus require a hefty fee for shipping the gold out.

Oh, the irony. The cost of living in town is so high that McCullough has to take on the job of sheriff so he can earn enough money to move on. But of course he's wildly successful in the job, works up the wrath and ire of the Danby patriarch as a result, and at the climax of the film the sheriff is attacked by scores of Danbys while the townsfolk turn their backs on their hapless sheriff.

After a brief crisis in which he considers heading for Australia after all, naturally McCullough saves the day, gets some laughs when he blows up the town brothel revealing many civic leaders enjoying their time there, and then gets the girl. It's a parody that's not a parody and a comic movie that gets it all right.

The Kentuckian

1955; directed by Burt Lancaster; screenplay by A. B. Guthrie Jr., based on the novel *The Gabriel Horn* by Felix Holt; starring Burt Lancaster, Dianne Foster, Una Merkel, and Walter Matthau

Based on a novel called *The Gabriel Horn,* Burt Lancaster's only directorial outing tells the story of a widower bound for Texas with his young son in the 1820s. Big Eli Wakefield (Lancaster) and his son Little Eli (Donald MacDonald) are looking for a fresh start in the wide-open frontier—the beginning of many a classic Western saga. And naturally the bad guys and beautiful women get in their way.

Walter Matthau made his screen debut as the villainous storekeeper, and Bond Girl Dianne Foster fills the role of the beautiful but down-on-her-luck indentured servant admirably. Father and son use their "Texas money" to buy her freedom and then have to earn it back while facing down a corrupt constable, wading through the intrigue of a long-standing family feud, and fending off a schoolteacher, Susie (Diana Lynn), who wants Big Eli to marry her and settle down.

There's a lot of action, a solid screenplay, and great glimpses at American history. And, of course, the heroes learn that the road to Texas isn't an easy one—but they stay true to their convictions and hold on to their dreams nonetheless.

APPENDIX A: HONORABLE MENTIONS

Oh, how we wished this book would accommodate the 112 Greatest Westerns of All Time, but that just didn't look as good on the dust jacket. Still, we feel we'd be remiss if we didn't mention this group of films, some well known, some you may never have heard of.

1. *The Man Who Loved Cat Dancing,* 1973, directed by Richard C. Sarafian, starring Burt Reynolds and Sarah Miles. This movie borrows a lot from the other films included on our list of the top one hundred, but it also takes a deeper look at relationships than some.

2. *Bite the Bullet,* 1975, directed by Richard Brooks, starring Gene Hackman, Candice Bergen, and James Coburn. A group of ex-Rough Riders, an ex-prostitute, and a gunfighter enter a horse race in the desert.

3. *Man without a Star,* 1955, directed by King Vidor, starring Kirk Douglas and Jeanne Crain. A cowboy goes to work for a hard-hearted lady rancher as her top hand and enforcer.

4. *Riders in the Sky,* 1949, directed by John English, starring Gene Autry and Gloria Henry. Gene Autry spins a classic yarn about the wrongly accused Ralph Lawson and the quest to clear his name as the back story to his song about "Ghost Riders in the Sky."

5. *Heartland,* 1979, directed by Richard Pearce, starring Rip Torn and Conchata Ferell. Letters written by pioneer Elinore Pruitt Stewart from 1909 to 1913 about her homesteading life are the basis for this survival story.

6. *Nevada Smith,* 1966, directed by Henry Hathaway, starring Steve McQueen. Nevada Smith is a half-breed bent on revenge after his father is killed—and this movie is filled with action but is also a keen study of the aftermath of a haunting incident.

7. *Laurel and Hardy Way Out West,* 1937, directed by James W. Horne, starring

Stan Laurel and Oliver Hardy. Stan and Ollie are on a mission to deliver the deed to a valuable gold mine to a naïve ingénue. The music in this fun movie was nominated for the Academy Award for Best Score.

8. *Django,* 1966, directed by Sergio Corbucci, starring Franco Nero. In this gorgeous, overshadowed spaghetti Western, the lonely Django rescues Maria from a group of bandits and arrives in a not-quite-ghost town, where only the saloon and the brothel are open.

9. *The Great Northfield, Minnesota Raid,* 1972, directed by Philip Kaufman, starring Cliff Robertson and Robert Duvall. It's based on the true story of the bungled robbery of the bank in the now sweet college town of Northfield, Minnesota.

10. *The Outlaw,* 1943, directed by Howard Hughes and Howard Hawks, starring Jane Russell. Pat Garrett, Doc Holliday, and Billy the Kid all make appearances, but Jane Russell and her cleavage steal the show. Don't take it too seriously, and you'll love it.

11. *The Hanging Tree,* 1959, directed by Delmer Daves, starring Gary Cooper. A doctor saves a young man from the mob trying to hang him, but goes on to control his life. Based on the novel by Dorothy M. Johnson.

12. *The Great Train Robbery,* 1903, directed by Edwin S. Porter, starring Gilbert M. "Broncho Billy" Anderson. It's a simple story: A group of bandits stages a train hold-up and is pursued by a posse. But it's the first narrative movie—and it's a *Western* with the first real cowboy star.

APPENDIX B: EXPLORE THE CINEMATIC WEST

BY DAN GAGLIASSO FOR *AMERICAN COWBOY*

Want to add some marquee moments to your Western travel experience? Take our show-stopping tour of the real-life places where your favorite Western movie scenes were shot.

Those magical moments—they live forever. Moments of cinematic splendor, as heroes and heroines, backdropped by the most magnificent Western vistas ever filmed, played out scenes that will always be a part of the American experience. The classic Western films had it all—romance, high adventure, drama, history, ruggedness, passion, action, suspense—and beauty. And what made it all the more beautiful was the world's greatest stage—the American West itself.

It can all come back to life again. Those places are still out there. And because they're in the West, most are still unspoiled. Someone looking for travel destinations couldn't ask for more—it was these incredible places that first attracted the film scouts of old, and that bring new filmmakers still. Perhaps no places on earth are more picturesque.

We've gone back and rediscovered the magic that was our favorite Westerns. You can, too. Come along as we visit the locations that brought the magic to life.

MONUMENT VALLEY, ARIZONA/UTAH, FORT APACHE

Visit Ford's Point and other sites in this classic Western locale.

John Ford was the motion picture director who, more than any other, recognized the importance of the land. "The real star of my Westerns is the land. A Western is all about the land." So said Ford during the filming of his last major Western, *Cheyenne Autumn,* in Monument Valley.

Ford wasn't the first director to film in Monument Valley, but seven of his greatest Westerns, starting with *Stagecoach* in 1939 and continuing through *Cheyenne Autumn* in 1964, established the red-rock mesas and spires as Ford's personal celluloid domain.

The valley is approximately five hours northeast of Flagstaff, Arizona. Route 163 is the only way into the valley from either

Arizona or Utah, and many of the sites of some of Ford's greatest scenes from films like *Fort Apache, She Wore a Yellow Ribbon,* and *The Searchers* are on both the Utah and Arizona sides of the state line. There is a small charge per person to drive into the valley that may be the best tourist deal in America.

Your first stop should be either the visitor's center or Goulding's Lodge (www .gouldings.com). Western film historians agree that it was the late Indian trader Harry Goulding who singlehandedly brought Monument Valley to John Ford's attention during the preproduction of the classic *Stagecoach* in 1939, though John Wayne had briefly filmed here on *The Big Trail* in 1930. Goulding's is where Ford, Wayne, and the other major stars would stay during production in the valley, and the updated quarters are not only the best place for a Western fan to stay, but also where several key scenes in Ford's Westerns were filmed. Goulding's also features extensive photographs and a museum on the classic Ford films shot here.

The old trading post and motel buildings at Goulding's were featured as the buildings of Fort Starke in Ford's classic cavalry film *She Wore a Yellow Ribbon* in 1949. Have a

Panavision moment by venturing a few scenic miles to where the fort's front walls, gate, and blockhouses were constructed several miles away, against a backdrop of Castle Butte to the left and West Mitten Butte to the right, atop a sharp rise. Careful use of camera angles allowed the crew to intercut these scenes with those back at Goulding's to make it all seem like one location.

This same area where Fort Starke was built is also where the cemetery scene in perhaps the greatest Western ever made, *The Searchers* (1954), was set. Stand on the rising slope where Wayne and Texas Ranger captain and minister Ward Bond buried Ethan Edward's family after the Comanche raid and you just might hear the echo of Wayne's voice warning, "That'll be the day!" The Edwards ranch site is back on the Utah side, in the distance. All you have to do is match up Sentinel Mesa to your right.

Southeast of Goulding's is Rock Door Canyon, the site of Henry Fonda's Custer-like cavalry charge in *Fort Apache.* There's a decent road right down the middle of the canyon where Fonda's cavalry charged to glory and a little further on near the rest center and parking area you'll notice the long mesa that was the background for "Thursday's last stand."

Off to the northeast on the Utah side up Highway 163 is the San Juan River at Mexican Hat that was used for various river crossings in *She Wore a Yellow Ribbon, The Searchers,* and *Cheyenne Autumn.* The surprising thing about the valley is just how close so many of these red rock landmarks are to each other. No matter which way you turn you'll recognize a mesa or a rock spire from *Stagecoach, My Darling Clementine,* and other Ford films.

Perhaps the most incredible spot in the whole valley is the appropriately named Ford Point. It's easy to see why Ford used this long, wide pedestal that surveys nearly the entire valley to such great effect. It is from here that Wayne's Ethan Edwards and the Texas Rangers finally discover Chief Scar's Comanche village at the climax of *The Searchers.* It's also the same spot where Richard Widmark's troop of cavalry halts, searching aimlessly for Dull Knife's Cheyenne in *Cheyenne Autumn.*

Just fifteen miles from Moab lies the Colorado River and, beside it, Arches National Park, along with a picturesque spread called Red Cliffs Ranch, where numerous great Westerns were filmed.

Colin Fryer, owner of the ranch and its resort, the Red Cliffs Lodge (www.redcliffs lodge.com), says one of the first stops for film buffs should be the resort's film museum. "It's full of memorabilia from the Westerns made here, as well as thousands of photographs," Fryer says.

Of course the resort itself, set amidst two-thousand-foot red sandstone cliffs, is enough draw in its own right. Says Fryer: "Imagine a ranch at the bottom of the Grand Canyon. That's what we are like. Visitors are amazed at the wide open spaces, especially if they are from Europe."

Some of the most important scenes of *Rio Grande* were filmed here, with the Colorado serving as proxy for the namesake river. Ford and his casts and crew would work Monument Valley and then come to this site for the Colorado River and the scenes it would afford.

And no jaunt through movie-rich Utah would be complete without a visit to Kanab, in the southwestern corner of the state (www.visitkanab.com). Jackie Hamblin Rife, a former stunt double who now works at a visitor's center in Kanab, says that film-related tourism to the area has been on the upswing. "People come from all over the world," she says.

OLD TUCSON

At the southern end of Arizona lies the state's other big movie-location draw—the still-active Old Tucson movie set. Long known as "Hollywood in the Desert," Old Tucson draws some 200,000 visitors per year, according to Maria Demarais, the site's marketing manager. Among the attractions are staged gunfights, stunt shows, musical shows in the saloon, and even a few kiddie rides (during the summer months). But the biggest pull is the movie history. This is where scores of classics were filmed, including *Winchester '73, Gunfight at the O.K. Corral, Rio Bravo, Cimarron* (the 1959 version), *Hombre, The Outlaw Josey Wales,* and *Tombstone.* Find out more at www.old tucson.com.

THE BLACK HILLS, SOUTH DAKOTA
Adventures still await where epics unfolded.

When Kevin Costner made the Academy Award–winning Best Picture *Dances with Wolves* in 1989, he wanted the film to have an authentic look and feel, so he set his sights on several areas in and around South Dakota's Black Hills. The Cinerama epic *How the West Was Won* also filmed major sequences here, especially the spectacular buffalo stampede, back in 1961. The commercial buffalo ranches where *Dances* hunting scenes were filmed are private businesses that cannot accommodate tourists, though you can see plenty of buffalo roaming free in Custer State Park . . . just keep your distance.

Five miles south of Rapid City on Highway 16 is the Fort Hays set where Costner's Lt. Dunbar gets his orders to travel to distant Fort Sedgwick. The three main buildings—including the major's quarters, the blacksmith shop, and the supply building—were relocated a short distance away from the original site and now house a gift shop, museum, and chuck wagon serving breakfast and dinner.

The winter campsite of the Lakotas, where Costner and his co-star Mary Mac-Donnell leave the Sioux at the end of the film, is further north near the charming little town of Spearfish. It's a three-mile hike through public land up Spearfish Canyon from the Spearfish Canyon Lodge parking lot, and a sign, sometimes the victim of light-fingered souvenir hunters, often marks the spot. The freight wagon journey to Fort Sedgwick was filmed at several spots in the Sage Creek Wilderness Area in Badlands National Park east of Rapid City and south of the famous Wall Drug on Interstate 90.

WILD HORSE SANCTUARY, HOT SPRINGS, SOUTH DAKOTA

Several years ago I directed a History Channel show called *Comanche Warrior* at this great location. Now, there weren't ever any Comanches in South Dakota, but Texas and Oklahoma didn't have any Comanche re-enactor types, so we transformed a group of modern Lakota horsemen into the "Lords of the Southern Plains." Disney's *Hidalgo* (2004) also filmed a few of its Dakota-based scenes here, and all of TNT's TV movie *Crazy Horse* (1996) was filmed here as well.

The Wild Horse Sanctuary is just a few miles south of Hot Springs and one hour south of Rapid City. It's a spectacular area with wide canyons, high bluffs, shallow riverbeds, and five hundred wild horses, both rescued domestics and feral mustangs.

Susan Watt, program director for the sanctuary, says that the site was another of the locations for *Dances with Wolves.* Most recently they hosted a German documentary team that was filming for *1491*, a look at what the Americas were like before the arrival of Columbus. (See www.wildmustangs .com.)

TATANKA AND JAKE'S, DEADWOOD, SOUTH DAKOTA

Just a mile north of Deadwood on Highway 85 is Kevin Costner's museum and buffalo statue tribute, dubbed Tatanka. A small but top-quality museum tells the story of the Lakota and the buffalo and is staffed with local Lakota experts. The site also features a spectacular group of larger-than-life-size bronzes of a mounted Lakota buffalo hunt (www.storyofthebison.com).

Back in Deadwood on Main Street is Jake's restaurant, atop the Midnight Star Casino, named after Costner's character in Silverado. Jake's is probably the finest restaurant between Billings and Sioux Falls. For sightseers there are great displays of Costner's movie costumes and memorabilia from *Dances with Wolves, Open Range, Silverado,* and *Wyatt Earp* in Diamond Lil's sports bar below Jake's (www.themidnight star.com).

BRACKETTVILLE, TEXAS
Stroll the sets of classic western movie-making.

What does John Wayne have in common with the classic Western miniseries *Lonesome Dove*? Two things. It seems that Larry McMurtry's original story was going to be a feature film called *Streets of Laredo,* to be produced in the late 1960s. John Wayne, James Stewart, and Henry Fonda would have played the three former Texas Rangers. The film never happened, so McMurtry later developed the screenplay into the award-winning novel. Second, key parts of *Lonesome Dove* were filmed at Alamo Village near Brackettville, Texas, the site of John Wayne's standing set for his 1960 epic *The Alamo.* The actual town of Lonesome Dove was built on the nearby Texas/Mexico border at the Rio Grande River on the Moody Ranch. The ranch is a working cattle operation and unfortunately can't accommodate sightseers.

Alamo Village is just seven miles north of Brackettville, which lies 140 miles west of San Antonio. It still ranks as the largest standing film set in the United States. There's a charge for entering. If filming is going on, you'll get more than your money's worth. There are also eighteen different film-related displays and exhibits.

The Alamo was John Wayne's dream project, his personal tribute to the courage that helped settle early Texas. He produced and directed the $12 million epic, risking a lot of his own personal fortune in the process. The mission/fortress and an 1830s representation of San Antonio were constructed as permanent sets on Happy Shahan's eighteen-thousand-acre ranch. More than a thousand costumed extras refought the famous battle here for two months back in late 1959.

It's a grand set. I worked on it myself back in 1986 on the Sam Elliott CBS TV movie *Houston—the Legend of Texas.* I'll never forget a group of us sitting atop the Alamo's front gate one night when a jokester in the shadows outside called out, "Hey, amigos! A message for Jeem Boow-ie. In the sombrer-ooo!," emulating a dramatic nighttime moment in the Wayne film. We all knew the line by heart and cracked up in unison. A number of other films have shot in the immediate area, including *Arrowhead* (1953) with Charlton Heston, as well as *Two Rode Together* (1960) and *Bandolero* (1967), both starring James Stewart.

Wayne's version of Alamo events may not be quite as modern as the 2004 Disney film *The Alamo,* which was a box office disaster, and Davy Crockett's manner of death is still a matter of unsettled debate, but the Wayne version of events is far more entertaining and satisfying. The magnificent set was as much one of the stars of the film as Wayne, Richard Widmark, and

Lawrence Harvey were—another dimension that the Duke grasped better than the latest Alamo filmmakers. Though altered for dozens of other Westerns, including *Lonesome Dove,* the real-adobe fortress and town can be explored by visitors. Alamo Village also boasts a substantial herd of authentic Texas longhorn cattle.

For *Lonesome Dove,* producer and writer Bill Wittliff easily figured out that he could film within the walls of the Alamo fortress as Robert Duvall's Gus and Tommy Lee Jones's Call ride past the reconstructed chapel as if it is now part of the burgeoning city center of 1870s San Antonio. As they ride past the cradle of Texas liberty, Gus opines, "Woodrow, if a thousand Comanch' had wiped us out in a gully like the Sioux just done Custer, they'd be writin' songs about us for a hundred years."

The fiftieth anniversary of the filming of Wayne's *The Alamo* and the creation of Alamo Village was in 2009, and the village celebrated Texas style with an outdoor showing of the 1960 epic on a large screen right in the Alamo compound. But it's still a worthwhile stop even without the festivities (www.alamovillage.com).

FORT CLARK SPRINGS

One unique place to stay in the area is the old cavalry post of Fort Clark, right down Highway 90 in Brackettville. This wonderful old historic army post dates from the 1850s. You get to stay in the old barracks rooms that are updated but still evocative of their Western military heritage. This is where John Wayne and his Alamo film crew stayed in 1959 during filming and it served as the main set during the filming of the Heston film *Arrowhead.* The restaurant serves great mesquite-grilled pork chops (www .fortclark.com).

JACKSON HOLE, WYOMING

The grand Tetons prove to be a picture-perfect backdrop.

Next to Monument Valley, perhaps no other Western film location comes up in conversation more than Wyoming's Grand Tetons, site of director George Steven's classic *Shane* (1953). Stevens had a secret weapon when he brought his film crew up to Jackson Hole in 1952—Charlie Russell's lone protégé, Joe De Yong. De Yong traveled all over the West with Stevens looking for a suitable location and in Grand Teton National Park and its environs they found just what they were looking for. The story was an amalgam of the themes present in the Johnson County Cattle War, and the massive Tetons offered a rugged and awe-inspiring backdrop to the simple yet powerful story. Two decades before, John Wayne had worked on his first starring film in the Tetons in the spectacular wagon train epic *The Big Trail* (1930). Howard Hawks's mountain man film *The Big Sky* also filmed here in 1951.

The settlement of Grafton's was constructed as a rustic, one-sided set in the tradition of Charlie Russell on the Antelope Flats, near Kelly and the Gros Ventre River, with the three Tetons towering in the background. Almost all of the town buildings were torn down many years ago. Kelly Warm Springs, near the National Elk Refuge, was the idyllic site for the exteriors of Van Heflin's Starrett homestead. One of the film's buildings, Ernie Wright's homesteader cabin, still remains, though in a state of advanced disrepair. I filmed part of a "history of hunting" documentary around the rustic Cunningham cabin in the early 1990s that was featured in the CBS miniseries *Dreams West* (1986).

Most of these areas are not directly accessible right from your car. You have to get out and walk, and I do mean walk. East Boundary Road off the park's main entrance will get you the closest to the general area of many of the bigger scenes in the film, such as Cemetery Hill, the burial spot of Torrey (Elisha Cooke Jr.). The Jackson Hole Historical Society has a nice exhibit on *Shane* and features the lone surviving building from the town of Grafton—the saddlery and harness shop.

Shane *Expert Walt Farmer*
Probably no one knows more about the making of *Shane* and its locations than Wyoming resident Walt Farmer. He's put out an impressive CD book that's well worth ordering if you're going to make the pilgrimage. It even has GPS coordinates for the locations. It can be ordered at www.theastrocowboy .com and sells for $20 including shipping.

RIDGEWAY AND OURAY, COLORADO
Tread streets that Wayne trod—amidst picturesque beauty.
John Wayne finally won a well-deserved Academy Award for his portrayal of the crusty U.S. Marshal Rooster Cogburn in *True Grit,* a 1969 film that still ranks as a fan favorite. *True Grit*'s director, Henry Hathaway, had shot parts of *How the West Was Won* in the area back in 1961 and knew what the surrounding mountains and

meadows—only fifty miles from the Continental Divide—could offer. So the beautiful little mountain town of Ridgway at the foot of the San Juan Mountains in southern Colorado on Highway 550 was transformed into 1880s Fort Smith, Arkansas.

In six weeks in 1968, the film's art director and his crew turned five blocks of the center of the old railroad town into Fort Smith, complete with Hanging Judge Parker's three-man gallows. The exterior of the red brick courthouse in nearby Ouray was duplicated in Ridgway while the interiors of the room were filmed inside the real courthouse. Most of the film's false-front period buildings were torn down after filming finished, though the firehouse now survives as an artist studio and the livery stable is now the post office. This friendly town still exhibits tremendous pride in Wayne and the film.

Ten miles west of Ridgway on Last Dollar Road is the old-style ranch that served as Kim Darby's Mattie's Ranch. While it is privately owned, no one minds if people pull over to snap a few pictures, and much of the ranch retains its *True Grit* look and feel. This is where, at the end of the film, Wayne's Rooster proclaims, "Well, come see an old fat man sometime!" as he gamely jumps his horse over the fence with a flourish of his hat.

Immediately west of town is Katie's Meadow, the Aspen-lined valley where Cogburn really proved what true grit he had. It is here in response to Robert Duvall's outlaw taunt that Wayne pulls his Colt revolver, cocks his Winchester, puts his horse's reins in his teeth and hollers, "Fill your hand, you son-of-a-bitch!" No wonder the only choice by the book's author (Charles Portis) to play Rooster was Wayne. If you contact the Ridgway Chamber of Commerce they'd be happy to provide you with a printed tour guide to the *True Grit* locations from the original John Wayne movie (www.ridgwaycolorado .com).

ABOUT *AMERICAN COWBOY* MAGAZINE

American Cowboy magazine was founded in 1994 and is based in Boulder, Colorado, www .americancowboy.com. It celebrates the authentic Western lifestyle with in-depth personality profiles, travel stories, and event coverage—including articles on the great Western movie genre. Part of Active Interest Media since 2003, the magazine also features artistic pictorials of Western landscapes and stories on cowboy gear, ranch know how, and history.

Philip Armour is the Editor-in-Chief